William Fleming

The true church of the Bible

William Fleming

The true church of the Bible

ISBN/EAN: 9783741178498

Manufactured in Europe, USA, Canada, Australia, Japa

Cover: Foto ©Lupo / pixelio.de

Manufactured and distributed by brebook publishing software (www.brebook.com)

William Fleming

The true church of the Bible

THE TRUE CHURCH

OF

THE BIBLE.

Part I.
INSTRUCTIONS FOR ANGLICANS AND DISSENTERS.

Part II.
INSTRUCTIONS FOR JEWS AND UNITARIANS.

BY
THE REV. W. FLEMING, M.R.

LONDON:
R. WASHBOURNE,
18 PATERNOSTER ROW, LONDON.
1895.

Nihil obstat:
WILLIAM L. GILDEA, D.D.

Imprimatur:
✠ HERBERT CARDINAL VAUGHAN,
ARCHBISHOP OF WESTMINSTER.

THIS LITTLE BOOK

IS AFFECTIONATELY DEDICATED

TO

ROBERT MILLS, ESQ.,

AS A SMALL TOKEN OF MANY KINDNESSES

RECEIVED BY THE AUTHOR.

PREFACE.

CHRIST founded a Church — one Church, and one Church only. This is a fact acknowledged by all Christians. The Bible, all equally acknowledge, points out, in clear decisive terms, the nature and characteristics of that Church. All Christians, no matter how widely they differ in religion, claim for the particular Church of which they are members the title of the Church of Christ — *the True Church of the Bible.* It is self-evident all cannot be right. It follows, then, that millions of Christians must be living in error — millions that fondly and firmly believe that theirs is the true Church of the Bible.

To help these to see their error is the object of the writer of the following pages. Knowing the suspicion with which Protestants regard the Catholic translation of the Sacred Scriptures, he has used the Anglican version, in the hope that these pages will be studied by them, and that, being convinced by proofs drawn from their own translation of the Bible that the Church of Rome is the one Church founded by Christ—the true Church of the Bible—they will not hesitate, in spite of all human ties that may have to be broken, in spite of all the sacrifices that may have to be made, to enter and become members of that Church in which alone is salvation and life eternal.

CONTENTS.

PART I.

CHAPTER I.

THERE IS BUT ONE TRUE FAITH.   PAGE

I. Christ's Mission on Earth to give one Faith to the whole World.   II. Christ's ardent Prayer for Unity of Faith amongst His Followers.   III. St. Paul's Doctrine as to the Necessity of Unity of Faith.   IV. The absolute Necessity of Unity of Faith proved by the Condemnation of Heretics.   V. Whether Heretics can be saved   1

CHAPTER II.

FAITH ALONE, AS PROTESTANTS TEACH, DOES NOT JUSTIFY.

I. What the Scripture means when it teaches that we are justified by any single Virtue.   II. Statement and Refutation of the Protestant Doctrine of Justification by Faith alone.   III. Answer to particular Difficulties and Objections   5

CHAPTER III.

THE PROTESTANT AND CATHOLIC RULES OF FAITH.

I. Explanation of the Protestant and Catholic rules of Faith.   II. Why Tradition should be admitted as a Rule of Faith.   III. The Protestant Rule of Faith, or private Interpretation of the Scriptures proved to be untenable   8

CHAPTER IV.

THERE IS BUT ONE TRUE CHURCH.   PAGE

I. One universal Church was founded by Christ for the Salvation of Men. II. He decreed that this Church should never fail, and made its teaching Body infallible. III. No true Christian can lawfully refuse to obey the Church 13

CHAPTER V.

THE PAPAL SUPREMACY.

I. St. Peter held the first Place of Honour in the Church. II. He was first in Power and Jurisdiction. III. The Pope, as successor to Peter, the first Pope and Bishop of Rome, inherits by right the Primacy of Honour and Jurisdiction over the universal Church 15

CHAPTER VI.

THE INFALLIBILITY OF THE POPE.

I. What Papal Infallibility means. II. The Divine Wisdom deemed it necessary to appoint an Infallible Head to His Church, both in the Old and New Testaments. III. Scriptural Proof of Papal Infallibility. IV. Scriptural Objections to Infallibility 18

CHAPTER VII.

THE CATHOLIC CHURCH IS THE ONE TRUE CHURCH   23

CHAPTER VIII.

THE SACRAMENT OF HOLY ORDER.

I. Christ instituted a sacred Hierarchy of Bishops and Priests, distinct from Laics, to govern His Church. II. The Apostles ordained Priests and Bishops, who in turn ordained others. III. The Objections of Dissenters to the Sacrament of Holy Order. IV. The Celibacy of the Clergy 23

Contents.

CHAPTER IX.

THE SACRIFICE OF THE MASS.

I. What the Mass really is. II. The Mass is the Sacrifice foretold by the Prophet Malachi. III. Our Saviour's Priesthood was established to offer up a distinct Sacrifice of its own. IV. When was this Sacrifice inaugurated? V. St. Paul said Mass. VI. Mass said during the First Three Centuries. VII. The Mass in no way derogates from the all-sufficient Sacrifice of the Cross . 26

CHAPTER X.

WHY LATIN IS USED AT THE DIVINE SERVICE . 38

CHAPTER XI.

THE SACRAMENT OF THE EUCHARIST.

I. Christ promised that He would give Himself to the Faithful in the Blessed Eucharist. II. Our Saviour fulfilled His Promise at the Last Supper. III. The early Christians believed in the Real Presence when they received the Blessed Eucharist 39

CHAPTER XII.

NO NECESSITY FOR COMMUNICATING IN BOTH KINDS.

I. Proof from Scripture that there is no Necessity for the Faithful to receive Communion in both Kinds. II. Tradition testifies to the Sufficiency of receiving Communion in one Kind alone. III. Objections answered. IV. The Real Presence taught by the Fathers of the First Three Centuries 44

CHAPTER XIII.

THE SACRAMENT OF BAPTISM.

I. Christ instituted this Sacrament. II. It is absolutely necessary that Children, as well as Adults, should be baptized. III. Baptism by Immersion is not necessary. IV. What is the Fate of Infants and Heathens, who have faithfully observed the natural Law, who die unbaptized? 48

CHAPTER XIV.

THE SACRAMENT OF PENANCE.

I. Institution of this Sacrament by Christ. II. The Apostles excercised the Power of forgiving Sins conferred on them by Christ. III. Confession of Sin was practised both in the Old and in the New Testament. IV. Confession during the First Three Centuries . 51

CHAPTER XV.

INDULGENCES.

I. The Meaning of an Indulgence. II. A certain amount of temporal Punishment frequently remains due to Sin when its Guilt has been forgiven. III. Our Saviour gave to St. Peter, and to the Apostles and their Successors, Power to remit both the Guilt of Sin, and also its temporal Punishment, for a reasonable cause. IV. By the 'Communion of Saints' the superabundant Merits of Christ and His Saints may be applied to the Faithful in the form of Indulgences 55

CHAPTER XVI.

PURGATORY.

I. All who admit a Difference between the Guilt of Venial and Mortal Sin are bound to admit a Difference in degree of Punishment due to these Sins in the next Life. II. The Jews believed in Purgatory. III. Why we pray for the Dead. IV. Prayers for the Dead in the Second and Third Centuries 58

CHAPTER XVII.

PENITENTIAL GOOD WORKS.

I. Works of Penance prescribed in the Old Testament. II. Penitential Good Works inculcated by our Lord and the Apostles 62

CHAPTER XVIII.

THE SACRAMENT OF EXTREME UNCTION.

I. The Truth of this Sacrament proved from Scripture. II. The Apostles anointed the Sick. III. The Benefits of this Sacrament 63

CHAPTER XIX.

THE BLESSED VIRGIN MARY.

I. The Blessed Virgin should be honoured by Christians more than any of the Angels or Saints. II. Mary was always a Virgin. III. The Immaculate Conception of the Blessed Virgin. IV. The Assumption of the Blessed Virgin 63

CHAPTER XX.

THE ANGELS.

I. Different Apparitions of Angels to Men. II. Guardian Angels. III. Angels should be honoured. IV. Angels know what passes on earth; they bless and pray for us 68

CHAPTER XXI.

SAINTS.

I. Meaning of the Name 'Saint.' II. Saints, whether in Heaven or on Earth, can pray for us. III. The Intercession of the Saints is not opposed to the Mediatorship of Christ. IV. St. Cyprian's exhortation to pray for one another after Death 71

CHAPTER XXII.

THE HOLY CROSS AND SACRED RELICS.

I. The Relics of the Saints should be honoured, and may be the occasion of God's working Miracles. II. Miracles did not cease at the Death of the Apostles . . . 74

CHAPTER XXIII.

SACRED IMAGES 75

CHAPTER XXIV.

THE SACRAMENTALS 77

PART II.

CHAPTER I.

THE BLESSED TRINITY.   PAGE

I. The Doctrine of the Blessed Trinity. II. Taught in the Old Testament. III. And in the Scriptures of the New Testament. IV. The Divine Persons are each one of them said to be God 82

CHAPTER II.

THE INCARNATION OF GOD THE SON.

I. The true Doctrine of the Incarnation of God the Son. II. The Opponents of the Doctrine of the Incarnation. III. The Messiah of the Jews is called by the Name of God. IV. St. John's Refutation of the Errors of the Docetæ, Cerinthians, and Ebionites. V. An Answer to the Doctrine of the Unitarians, who teach that Christ had no eternal Existence as God before He was born of the Virgin Mary 86

CHAPTER III.

THE HISTORY OF THE MESSIAH AS FORETOLD BY THE PROPHETS.

I. The Genealogy of the Messiah. II. The Time fixed for His coming by the Prophets. III. The Place where He should be born. IV. His public Life and Miracles. V. The Circumstances which should attend His Death. VI. The subsequent Events which should take place . 93

CHAPTER IV.

JESUS CHRIST IDENTIFIED AS THE MESSIAH.

I. The Genealogies of Christ and the Messiah correspond. II. The Time of Christ's Coming corresponds with the Date fixed by the Prophets. III. Our Saviour born at Bethlehem. IV. Christ's public Life identical with that prophesied of the Messiah. V. The Circumstances attending His Death are identical. VI. And also the subsequent Events 100

APPENDIX 107

THE TRUE CHURCH
OF
THE BIBLE.

PART I.
Instructions for Anglicans and Dissenters.

CHAPTER I.
THERE IS BUT ONE TRUE FAITH.

I. *Christ's mission on earth to give One Faith to the whole world.*

THE high-priest Caiaphas, inspired by the Holy Ghost, announced to the astonished priests and Pharisees assembled in council that it was necessary that Christ should die, to save and unite all the nations of the earth in one faith.

Caiaphas, being high-priest, 'said unto them: Ye know nothing at all' (John, xi. 49).

'Nor consider that it is expedient for us that one Man should die for the people, and that the whole nation perish not' (John, xi. 50).

'And this he spake not of himself, but, being high-priest that year, he prophesied that Jesus should die for that nation' (John, xi. 51).

'And not for that nation' (the Jewish) 'only, but

that also He should gather together in one' (faith) 'the children of God that were scattered' (the Gentiles) (John, xi. 52). This was our Saviour's expressed intention.

'Other sheep I have, which are not of this fold; them also I must bring, and they shall hear My voice: and there shall be óne fold and one shepherd' (John, x. 16).

II. *Christ's ardent prayer for unity of faith amongst His followers.*

Just before His death He prayed to His eternal Father to grant unity to the Apostles in teaching, and to the faithful in believing, that faith which He Himself had taught:

'And now I am no more in the world; but these are in the world, and I come to Thee. Holy Father, keep through Thine own name those whom Thou hast given Me, that they may be one, as We are' (John, xvii. 11).

'Neither pray I for these alone' (the Apostles), 'but for them also which shall believe on Me through their word' (John, xvii. 20).

'That they all may be one, as Thou, Father, in Me, and I in Thee, that they also may be one in Us: that the world may believe that Thou hast sent Me' (John, xvii. 21).

In other words, the union of the Apostles in teaching and of all the faithful in one faith was destined as a sign to convince the world of the truth of the Christian religion.

III. *St. Paul's doctrine as to the necessity of unity of faith.*

'He is our peace, who hath made both' (Jew and Gentile) 'one, and hath broken down the middle wall of partition between us'.(Eph. ii. 14).

'And that He might reconcile both unto God in one body by the Cross' (Eph. ii. 16).

'Now, therefore, ye are no more strangers and foreigners, but fellow-citizens with the saints, and of the household of God' (Eph. ii. 19).

'And are built upon the foundation of the Apostles and prophets, Jesus Christ Himself being the chief corner-stone' (Eph. ii. 20).

'There is one body and one spirit, even as ye are called to one hope of your calling' (Eph. iv. 4).

'One Lord, one faith, one baptism' (Eph. iv. 5).

'One God, the Father of all, who is about all, and through all, and in you all' (Eph. iv. 6).

In the 11th and 12th verses St. Paul states that the Apostles, Evangelists, pastors, and teachers were instituted that all Christians might come 'in the unity of the faith, and of the knowledge of the Son of God, unto a perfect man, unto the measure of the stature of the fulness of Christ' (Eph. iv. 13).

'That we henceforth be no more children, tossed to and fro, and carried about by every wind of doctrine, by the sleight of men and cunning craftiness, whereby they lie in wait to deceive' (Eph. iv. 14).

IV. *The absolute necessity of unity in faith proved by the condemnation of heretics.*

All who would still deny the necessity of unity in faith, affirming that it matters not which form of Christianity they profess, should read these terrible denunciations uttered against those who have departed from the unity of the true faith:

'But though we, or an angel from heaven, preach any other Gospel unto you than that which we have preached unto you, let him be accursed' (Gal. i. 8).

'As we said before, so say I now again, if any man preach any other Gospel unto you than that ye have received, let him be accursed' (Gal. i. 9).

Consistently with this, St. Paul requires Titus (iii. 10) to reject 'a man that is an heretic after the first and second admonition;' whilst he himself condemns Simon Magus (Acts, viii. 9, 10), Hymenæus and Alexander (1 Tim. i. 20), and 'delivered unto Satan' Hymenæus and Philetus (2 Tim. ii. 16, 17). The Nicolaitanes (Rev. ii. 6, 15) are accused of heresy by St. John, who calls heretics Antichrists (1 John, ii. 18, 19).

V. *Whether heretics can be saved.*

The Church, in anathematising and excommunicating those of her subjects who persist in teaching false doctrines, simply exercises that office conferred on her by Christ (Matt. xviii. 17; Luke, x. 16). It is her duty to guard the faithful from false teachers or heretics. There is nothing arbitrary or unreasonable in this exercise of power. If the doctrine of the supposed heretics be true, then the Church is in error, and its excommunication a benefit ; whereas, if heretics are in wilful error, they fully deserve the sentence of excommunication.

Whilst the Church has always taught that obstinate and wilful heretics, who err through malice, not through ignorance, cannot be saved, she has ever admitted that those who, brought up from infancy in false religions, are invincibly ignorant of the true faith can be saved if their good works correspond with their faith. This may be readily conceded, and is not inconsistent with the doctrine that there is but one true faith.

CHAPTER II.

FAITH ALONE, AS PROTESTANTS TEACH, DOES NOT JUSTIFY.

I. *What the Scripture means when it teaches that we are justified by any single virtue.*

THE Sacred Scripture, in stating that a man is justified by any single virtue, presupposes the existence of charity and other virtues, and only declares that the virtue mentioned as justifying is the operating or chief virtue at the time, by the exercise of which salvation may be gained.

The Sermon on the Mount will serve to illustrate what has been said (Matt. v. 3, *seq.*): 'The poor in spirit,' 'they that mourn,' 'thirst after righteousness,' 'the merciful,' 'the pure of heart,' 'peacemakers,' the 'reviled and persecuted,' are said to be justified. St. John (1 John, iii. 6) affirms that hope, Ezek. (xviii. 21) that penance, St. Luke (vii. 47) that charity, and, lastly, St. Paul (Gal. v. 14) that loving one's neighbour justifies. 'All the law is fulfilled in one word, even in this: Thou shalt love thy neighbour as thyself.' As it would evidently be perverting God's Word to assert any one of these virtues—say, loving one's neighbour—justifies to the exclusion even of faith, so, when faith is mentioned as justifying, it would be untrue to assert that we are justified by that virtue alone, to the exclusion of all others.

II. *Statement and refutation of the Protestant doctrine of justification by faith.*

Justification by faith, as many Protestants teach, does not imply that any moral change takes place in the soul of the person justified, but that the merits of Christ are applied to that soul, and though he who is justified by faith remain in sin, God will repute him as just. The faith by which such a one is justified is not a theological faith, or belief in all that God has revealed, but a personal faith, by which the man justified believes that the merits of Christ will be applied to him personally, and that, even though he persevere in sin, his salvation is secure.

St. Paul plainly refutes this doctrine:

'Though I should have the gift of prophecy, and understand all mysteries and all knowledge; and though I have all faith, so that I could remove mountains, and have not charity, I am nothing' (1 Cor. xiii. 2).

'And now abideth faith, hope, and charity, these three; but the greatest of these is charity' (1 Cor. xiii. 13).

The Apostle here mentions faith of every kind, individual and general—'all faith'—and absolutely declares that faith is useless without charity.

He affirms again the same truth:

'In Jesus Christ neither circumcision availeth anything, nor uncircumcision, but faith which worketh by love' (Gal. v. 6).

Faith, to merit justification, must be animated by charity, or love of God.

St. Augustine (*De Fide et Operibus*, cap. xiv.) tells us that St. James wrote his Epistle to correct those who falsely interpreted certain passages in St. Paul's Epistles. The Apostle argues with them in this way:

'Wilt thou know, O vain man, that faith without works is dead?' (James, ii. 20.)

'Was not Abraham our father justified by works, when he had offered Isaac his son on the altar?' (James, ii. 21.)

'Seest thou how faith wrought with his works, and by works was faith made perfect?' (James, ii. 22.)

'Ye see then how by works a man is justified, and not by faith only' (James, ii. 24).

Faith alone does not Justify.

'For as the body without the spirit is dead, so faith without works is dead' (James, ii. 26).

III. *Answer to particular difficulties and objections.*

The Catholic doctrine of faith gives us the solution of all difficulties. There are two kinds of faith—objective faith, which embraces all revealed doctrine; and subjective faith, which exists in the soul of the believer, and by which he believes in all that God has revealed. Subjective faith is the foundation of all virtues, and when vivified by charity renders all actions meritorious of supernatural reward; for good works without faith merit only a natural reward. Bearing this in mind, we can interpret St. Paul's saying:

'By grace are ye saved through faith: and that not of yourselves; it is the gift of God' (Eph. ii. 8).

'Not of works, lest any man should boast' (Eph. ii. 9).

St. Paul means faith influenced by charity (1 Cor. xiii. 2). Again, Protestants urge:

'We conclude that a man is justified by faith without the deeds of the law' (Rom. iii. 28).

The answer is evident! St. Paul speaks of the faith of Christ in opposition to the Jewish ceremonial law.

See the meaning of law as opposed to faith in John, i. 17, and Rom. vi. 14, 15.

Faith, then, must be animated by charity or perfected by works to be meritorious. Christ warns Christians that faith alone will not save them at the last day.

'Not every one that saith unto Me, Lord, Lord, shall enter into the kingdom of heaven, but he that doeth the will of My Father which is in heaven' (Matt. vii. 21).

'Many will say unto Me in that day: Lord, Lord,

have we not prophesied in Thy name? and in Thy name have cast out devils? and in Thy name done many wonderful works?' (Matt. vii. 22.)

'And then will I profess unto them: I never knew you. Depart from Me, ye that work iniquity' (Matt. vii. 23).

'Whosoever heareth these sayings of Mine, and doeth them, I will liken him unto a wise man that built his house upon a rock' (Matt. vii. 24).

'And every one that heareth these sayings of Mine, and doeth them not, shall be likened to a foolish man which built his house upon the sand' (Matt. vii. 26).

Such will be the reward of faith without charity or good works.

CHAPTER III.

THE PROTESTANT AND CATHOLIC RULES OF FAITH.

I. *Explanation of the Protestant and Catholic rules of faith.*

PROTESTANTS teach that we can only discover the true faith of Jesus by reading and interpreting for ourselves the Sacred Scriptures. Catholics, while, of course, accepting the Sacred Scriptures as the infallible Word of God, accept also and equally as the infallible Word of God the truths contained in Divine Tradition. By the truths of Divine Tradition we mean those articles of faith which though not contained in the Scriptures were nevertheless divinely revealed to the Apostles, and have been handed down by the living and infallible voice of the Church.

II. *Why Tradition should be admitted as a rule of faith.*

We may gather the reason from St. John:
'There are also many other things which Jesus

did, the which, if they should be written every one, I suppose that even the world itself could not contain the books which should be written' (John, xxi. 25).

Let it be remembered that St. John is the last of the Evangelists, and, with three other Gospels before his mind, makes this statement, and it will follow that the four Gospels give but an incomplete epitome of our Saviour's discourses and miracles. The Sacred Epistles scarcely dwell on either. We must look to tradition or the unwritten word for a fuller explanation of our holy faith, and we are warranted in doing this by the exhortations of St. Paul:

'Hold fast the form of sound words which thou hast heard of me' (2 Tim. i. 13).

'The things which thou hast heard of me, among many witnesses, the same commit thou to faithful men, who shall be able to teach others also' (2 Tim. ii. 2).

'Stand fast, and hold the traditions which ye have been taught, whether by word or our Epistle' (2 Thess. ii. 15).

It is, moreover, well known that St. Bartholomew taught the Gospel of Jesus Christ in Judea and Persia, St. Andrew in Scythia, St. Thomas in Parthia; and others of the Apostles preached the faith of Christ to the world, without the aid of the Scriptures of the New Testament.

Protestants must trust to tradition for a fuller explanation of the Blessed Trinity and of the mystery of the Incarnation, or of the procession of the Holy Ghost, than is given in the Sacred Scriptures. Where is their scriptural authority for changing the Sabbath to Sunday? Tradition is most useful in settling disputed points of doctrine. To give a few instances:

In the first century Clement is the acknowledged head of the Church, and condemns a heresy amongst the Corinthians (Eusebius, lib. iii. cap. xvi, and xxxviii.).

In this century St. Ignatius, speaking of the Docetæ, testifies to the truth of the Real Presence. 'They stay away from the Eucharist and prayer, because they will not acknowledge it to be the flesh of our Saviour Jesus Christ, that flesh which suffered for our sins' (*Epist. ad Smyrn.*).

'In the second century, St. Iræneus, (lib. iii. cap. iii.) speaks of the supremacy of the Roman See: 'For to this Church, on account of its superior headship, every other must have recourse, that is, the faithful of all nations.' This holy man calls the mass 'a pure sacrifice to God' (*Adv. Hæreses*, cap. xxxii.).

In the third century Origen in his Homilies speaks of the intercession of the Blessed Virgin, 'O woman blessed amongst women, we fly to thee.' And of her Immaculate Conception, 'She was never tainted by the serpent's poisonous breath' (Hom. vi. in Luc.).

St. Athanasius (*Serm. in Annunciatione*) invokes our Mother, 'Queen, Mother of God, pray for us;' 'Remember us, O most holy Virgin.'

These are the representative writers of the early Church, and, as their teaching is an unmistakable sign of the belief of the early Christians, we can fairly assume that they taught the true doctrines, handed down by tradition, on the subjects mentioned.

III. *The Protestant rule of faith, or private interpretation of the Scriptures, proved to be untenable.*

Such a rule of faith could not have been adopted by Christians before the art of printing was invented, that is for fifteen centuries, for during that period copies of the Sacred Scriptures could only be obtained in manuscript, and at enormous cost.

It must surely strike every Protestant who carefully studies the Sacred Scriptures, that our Saviour, neither directly or indirectly, foretold that the New Testament should be written, and, after the death of

Rules of Faith.   11

the Apostles, form the Christian's sole guide in faith; whilst, on the other hand, He insists on the Divine authority of the Church.

If private interpretation of the Sacred Scriptures be necessary to gain a knowledge of the true faith, how are the ignorant and unlettered in the present time to be instructed in the true religion?

Private interpretation of the Word of God was never allowed in the Old Testament, but the people looked up to the priests as their teachers in religion. This will be seen by consulting:

'Amariah, the chief priest, is over you in all matters of the Lord' (2 Chron. xix. 11).

The priests are commanded to 'teach the children of Israel all the statutes which the Lord hath spoken unto them by the hand of Moses' (Lev. x. 11).

The priests 'shall teach Jacob Thy judgments, and Israel Thy law' (Deut. xxxiii. 10).

'Ezra, the priest, brought the law before the congregation both of men and women, and all that could hear with understanding upon the first day of the seventh month' (Nehem. viii. 2).

'And Ezra opened the book in the sight of all the people (for he was above all the people); and when he opened it all the people stood up' (Nehem. viii. 5).

'And the Levites caused the people to understand the law' (Nehem. viii. 7).

The priests 'read in the book in the law of God distinctly, and gave the sense, and caused them to understand the reading' (Nehem. viii. 8).

'The priest's lips should keep knowledge, and they should seek the law at his mouth, for he is the messenger of the Lord of Hosts' (Mal. ii. 7).

The priests of the new law hold the same authority in Christ's Church, as is evident from Christ's words:

'Go ye therefore and teach all nations, baptizing them in the name of the Father, and of the Son, and of the Holy Ghost' (Matt. xxviii. 19).

'Teaching them to observe all things, whatsoever I have commanded you; and lo, I am with you alway, even unto the end of the world' (Matt. xxviii. 20).

All who refuse to obey their teaching are to be regarded:

'As an heathen man and a publican' (Matt. xviii. 17).

See likewise Luke, x. 16; Heb. xiii. 17; and—

'We are of God: he that knoweth God heareth us; he that is not of God heareth not us. Hereby know we the spirit of truth and the spirit of error' (1 John, iv. 6).

The faithful are warned that no prophecy or exposition of Scripture is of private interpretation:

'No prophecy of Scripture is of any private interpretation' (2 Peter, i. 20).

'For the prophecy came not in old time by the will of man, but holy men of God spake as they were moved by the Holy Ghost' (2 Peter, i. 20).

St. Paul exhorts the prophets or teachers of the new law:

'Having then gifts differing according to the grace that is given to us, whether prophecy, let us prophesy according to the proportion' (that is, according to the rule) 'of faith' (Rom. xii. 6).

The prophecy or teaching of the prophets of the new law must be in harmony with the teaching of the Church. Again, St. Peter warns the faithful:

'Our beloved brother Paul also, according to the wisdom given unto him, hath written unto you' (2 Pet. iii. 15).

'As also in all his Epistles, speaking in them of these things, in which are some things hard to be understood, which they that are unlearned and unstable wrest, as they do also the other Scriptures, unto their own destruction' (2 Pet. iii. 16).

'Ye therefore, beloved, seeing ye know these things before, beware lest ye also, being led away with the error of the wicked, fall from your own stedfastness' (2 Pet. iii. 17).

Christians, therefore, should make Scripture and tradition, as taught and interpreted by the Church, their rule of faith.

CHAPTER IV.

THERE IS BUT ONE TRUE CHURCH.

I. *One Universal Church was founded by Christ for the salvation of men.*

OUR Lord and the Apostles always teach that the Church is one:

'Upon this rock I will build My Church' (Matt. xvi. 18).

'If he neglect to hear them, tell it unto the Church' (Matt. xviii. 17).

'There shall be one fold and one Shepherd' (John, x. 16).

'Husbands, love your wives, even as Christ also loved the Church and gave Himself for it' (Eph. v. 25).

'That He might present it to Himself a glorious Church, not having spot or wrinkle' (Eph. v. 27).

'No man ever yet hateth his own flesh, but nourisheth and cherisheth it, even as the Lord the Church' (Eph. v. 29).

II. *He decreed that this Church should never fail, and made its teaching body infallible.*

'Thou art Peter, and upon this rock I will build My Church; and the gates of hell shall not prevail against it' (Matt. xvi. 18).

'Lo, I am with you alway, even unto the end of the world' (Matt. xxviii. 20).

'And I will pray the Father, and He will give you another Comforter, that He may abide with you for ever' (John, xiv. 16).

The first of these texts (Matt. xvi. 18) proves that the power of hell can never prevail against the Church; and from the last two (Matt. xxviii. 20 and John, xiv. 16) we gather that Jesus Christ and the Holy Ghost are ever present guarding the Church from error; for the words must refer to the successors of the Apostles, as the Apostles themselves could not live for ever.

This is further strengthened by the fact that the Apostles both ordained and transmitted their power to their successors. Thus Titus and Timothy are appointed Bishops of Crete and Ephesus by St. Paul:

'For this cause left I thee in Crete, that thou shouldest set in order the things that are wanting, and ordain elders in every city as I had appointed thee' (Titus, i. 5).

Timothy is appointed Bishop of Ephesus (1 Tim. i. 3), and commanded by St. Paul:

'Stir up the gift of God which is in thee by the putting on of my hands' (2 Tim. i. 6).

'That good thing which was committed unto thee keep by the Holy Ghost, which dwelleth in us' (2 Tim. i. 14).

St. Paul speaks again to the bishops of the Church:

'Take heed, therefore, unto yourselves, and to all the flock over the which the Holy Ghost hath made you overseers, to feed the Church of God, which He hath purchased with His own Blood' (Acts, xx. 28).

III. *No true Christian can lawfully refuse to obey the Church.*

Christ says of an obstinate Christian:

'If he neglect to hear the Church, let him be to thee as an heathen man and a publican' (Matt. xviii. 17).

He strengthens the authority of His disciples:
'He that heareth you heareth Me, and he that despiseth you despiseth Me' (Luke, x. 16).

SS. Paul and John preach the same doctrine:
'Obey them that have the rule over you, and submit yourselves; for they watch for your souls, as they that must give account' (Heb. xiii. 17).

'We are of God: he that knoweth God heareth us; he that is not of God heareth us not. Hereby know we the spirit of truth and the spirit of error' (1 John, iv. 6).

Whenever a dispute arises on a point of doctrine, the decision of the teachers of the Church, assembled in council, should guide the Christian's faith, even as the Apostles obeyed the infallible voice of St. Peter in the Council of Jerusalem, and issued the decree, 'It seemed good to the Holy Ghost and to us,' &c. (Acts, xv. 28), which fully testifies to the infallibility of the Church's teaching.

A Catholic's submission to the general teaching of the Church, as well as his firm faith in what has been defined by its head, is the logical result of his belief in our Saviour's words (Matt. xvi. 18; xxviii. 20; John, xiv. 16).

Finally, Jesus Christ has pledged that His Church can never fail, and the indwelling of the Holy Ghost is a guarantee that it can never fall into error.

CHAPTER V.

THE PAPAL SUPREMACY.

I. *St. Peter held the first place of honour in the Church.*

THE change of the name Simon to Peter, signifying the rock or foundation of the Church; the occurrence of his name as first in the list of the Apostles (Matt. x. 2, 3; Luke, vi. 14; Acts, i. 13); the position he holds in the election of Matthias (Acts, i.) and in the Council of Jerusalem (Acts, xv.) are sufficient to convince every one, who is not prejudiced, of the truth of what has been enunciated.

II. *He was first in power and jurisaiction.*

'And I say also unto thee, that thou art Peter, and upon this rock I will build My Church; and the gates of hell shall not prevail against it' (Matt. xvi. 18).

'And I will give unto thee the keys of the kingdom of heaven: and whatsoever thou shalt bind on earth shall be bound in heaven; and whatsoever thou shalt loose on earth shall be loosed in heaven' (Matt. xvi. 19).

'Jesus saith to Simon Peter: Simon, son of Jonas, lovest thou Me more than these? He saith unto Him: Yea, Lord, thou knowest that I love Thee. He saith unto him: Feed My lambs' (John, xxi. 15).

'He saith to him again the second time: Simon, son of Jonas, lovest thou Me? He saith unto Him: Yea, Lord, Thou knowest that I love Thee. He saith unto him: Feed My sheep' (John, xxi. 16).

'He saith unto him the third time: Simon, son of Jonas, lovest thou Me? Peter was grieved because He said unto him the third time: Lovest thou Me? And he said unto Him: Lord, Thou knowest all things; Thou knowest that I love Thee. Jesus saith unto him: Feed My sheep' (John, xxi. 17).

The power given by Christ to Peter of feeding the lambs and sheep implies the right of directing, governing, and teaching all the faithful. St. Peter himself uses a similar expression in exhorting the elders or priests to 'feed the flock of God which is among you, taking oversight thereof, not by constraint, but willingly' (1 Pet. v. 2; see also Acts, xx. 28).

Giving over the keys is symbolical, amongst all

The Papal Supremacy.

nations, of conferring power. Thus God speaks of the Messiah by the prophet:

'The key of the house of David will I lay upon His shoulder; and He shall open and none shall shut, and He shall shut and none shall open' (Isa. xxii. 22).

When our Saviour gave to Peter 'the keys of the kingdom of heaven, He appointed him the ruler of His Church, His kingdom upon earth' (Matt. xiii. 24, 31, 47).

III. *The Pope, as successor to Peter, the first Pope and Bishop of Rome, inherits by right the primacy of honour and jurisdiction over the universal Church.*

St. Peter established his episcopal see at Rome, and died there.

Some have denied that St. Peter was ever at Rome; but the learned Lardner, himself a Protestant, refutes this groundless assertion, and says: (*Can.* vol. iii. c. 18) 'This is the general, uncontradicted, disinterested testimony of ancient writers, Greeks, Latins, and Syrians. As our Lord's prediction concerning the death of Peter is recorded in one of the four Gospels, it is very likely that Christians would observe the accomplishment of it, which must have been in some place; and about this place there is no difference amongst Christian writers of ancient times. Never any other place was named besides Rome, nor did any other city ever glory in the martyrdom of Peter. It is not to our honour, nor to our interest, as Christians or Protestants, to deny the truth of events ascertained by early and well-attested tradition. If any make ill use of such facts we are not accountable for it; we are not, from dread of abuses, to overthrow the credit of all history, the consequences of which would be fatal.'

How is it that the Bishop of Rome holds the same office in the Church as St. Peter?

The answer to this question is apparent. Our

Saviour simply organized His Church when on earth, and showed in that organization the future mode of its government. He did not surely wish that the faithful, at the death of the Apostles, should be left in a state of spiritual helplessness and doubt. As the promise that He would be ever present with the Apostles to the end of the world (Matt. xxviii. 20), and that the Holy Ghost should 'abide with them for ever' (John, xiv. 16), must necessarily refer to their successors, so the promises made to, and the power conferred on, St. Peter are also fulfilled in him who has succeeded to his episcopate. If not, the Church does not rest securely on the rock on which it was founded, and its government by one pastor (John, x. 16) is at an end, and there is no longer 'one fold and one Shepherd,' but several disunited Churches which cannot last, as Christ assures us. 'Every kingdom divided against itself is brought to desolation' (Matt. xii. 25).

As it is an undisputed fact that bishops, not only in Catholic, but in Protestant, Churches, derive their authority and influence from the sees in which they are placed, the Bishop of Rome, possessing the see, holds the office of St. Peter in the Church. No other bishop, maintaining his former see, has ever been Pope; and from the foundation of Christianity the Bishop of Rome has been acknowledged by a vast majority of Christians to be the ruler of Christ's Church upon earth.

CHAPTER VI.

THE INFALLIBILITY OF THE POPE.

I. *What Papal Infallibility means.*

CATHOLICS believe that whenever that Sovereign Pontiff speaks *ex cathedrâ*, or solemnly, on the part of

The Infallibility of the Pope. 19

Christ's Church, on questions of faith or morals, the Holy Ghost, who always abides in the Church, will preserve him from giving an erroneous judgment. It does not imply that the Holy Father cannot sin, or err in conversation, or as a private doctor. His infallibility is limited, as will be seen by the following quotations :

'He speaks *ex cathedrâ*, or infallibly, when he speaks, first, as universal teacher; secondly, in the name and with the authority of the Apostles; thirdly, on a point of faith or morals; fourthly, with the purpose of binding every member of the Church to accept and believe his decision.'

Hence Billuart, speaking of the Pope, says: 'Neither in conversation, nor in discussion, nor in interpreting the Scriptures or the Fathers, nor in consulting, nor in giving his reasons for the point which he has defined, nor in answering letters, nor in private deliberations, supposing he is setting forth his own opinion, is the Pope infallible.' 'And for this simple reason, because on these occasions of speaking his mind he is not in the chair of the Universal Doctor' (Dr. Newman's Letter to the Duke of Norfolk, p. 129). 'Never,' says Perrone, 'have Catholics taught that the gift of infallibility is given by God to the Church after the manner of inspiration. Again (human) media of arriving at the truth are excluded neither by a Council's nor by a Pope's infallibility; for God has promised it, not by way of an infused' (or habitual) 'gift, but by way of assistentia' (Cardinal Newman's Letter to the Duke of Norfolk).

II. *The Divine Wisdom deemed it necessary to appoint an infallible head to His Church both in the Old and New Testament.*

The high-priest in Israel was respected as the supreme judge in all religious controversies. Whenever he was invested with 'Urim and Thummim,' or with truth and justice, and spoke from the oracle, God made known His Divine Will (Lev. viii. 8). For example: God commands Moses to take Joshua before Eleazar:

'He shall stand before Eleazar the priest, who shall ask counsel for him, after the judgment of Urim, before the Lord; at his word they shall go out, and at his word they shall come in, both he and all the children of Israel with him, even all the congregation' (Numb. xxvii. 21).

'In controversy they' (the priests) 'shall stand in judgment; and they shall judge according to My judgments' (Ezek. xliv. 24).

The difference between infallibility and impeccability is clearly indicated by our Lord:

'The scribes and Pharisees sit in Moses' seat' (Matt. xxiii. 2).

'All therefore whatsoever they bid you observe, that observe and do; but do not ye after their works, for they say and do not' (Matt. xxiii. 3).

'Caiaphas, being the high-priest that same year, saith unto them: Ye know nothing at all' (John, xi. 49).

'Nor consider that it is expedient for us that one man should die for the people, and that the whole nation perish not' (John, xi. 50).

'And this spake he not of himself; but being high-priest that year, he prophesied that Jesus should die for the nation' (John, xi. 51).

God in His wisdom made the high-priests individually, and the Levites in council, infallible, to preserve that ancient religion in its integrity; and He has likewise decreed that the ruler of His Church should be infallible, to preserve the Church, for which His Son died, from falling away from the unity of faith.

The Infallibility of the Pope.

III. *Scriptural proof of Papal Infallibility.*

'And I say unto thee, that thou art Peter, and upon this rock I will build My Church; and the gates of hell shall not prevail against it' (Matt. xvi. 18).

'And I will give unto thee the keys of the kingdom of heaven' (Matt. xvi. 19).

These texts equally prove that neither the Church founded by Christ, nor the foundation on which it rested, could ever fail. The words of Christ would be meaningless if the Church governed by Peter, or he in ruling it, could fall into error.

Our Lord spoke again on the same subject:

'Simon, Simon, behold Satan hath desired to have you, that he might sift you as wheat' (Luke, xxii. 31).

'But I have prayed for thee, that thy faith fail not; and when thou art converted, strengthen thy brethren' (Luke, xxii. 32).

He imposed on Peter the office of strengthening his brethern in the faith, and keeping them from error. St. Peter (Acts, xv. 7) claimed for himself the pre-eminent right of deciding the questions submitted to the Council of Jerusalem; and St. James (14) and the elders concurred at once in St. Peter's decision, in these words:

'It seemed good to the Holy Ghost and to us,' &c. (Acts, xv. 7, 10, 11, 14, 22, 28, 29).

It is Satan's dearest wish to lead the head of the Church into error, but this can never happen, owing to the prayer of Christ, 'I have prayed for thee,' &c. Christ, therefore, conferred on Peter that infallibility for which he prayed; and as He wished His Church to last for ever, and was then establishing the form of its government by one head (John, x. 16), He not only prayed for Peter, but in behalf of the future rulers of the Church, as the same necessity for infallibility remains.

IV. *Scriptural objections to Infallibility.*

It is urged that Peter's faith failed when he denied Christ. Our Saviour promised, but did not appoint Peter head of the Church before the Resurrection. The words, 'being once converted confirm thy brethren,' make known to us that the promise should not be fulfilled before Peter's fall (see John, xxi. 15).

Again, it is objected that St. Peter was rebuked by St. Paul (Gal. ii. 11-14).

The solution of this difficulty will be clearly seen, if it be borne in mind that, at the time mentioned, a controversy was raging between the Jewish and Gentile converts about the necessity of observing the Mosaic distinction of meats, and that St. Paul tells them both to yield to each other's weakness, when scandal would otherwise arise (Rom. xiv. 15, 20).

Mindful of the high feeling on both sides, and fearful of scandalising the Jewish converts—for he was their Apostle—St. Peter withdrew himself from the table of the Gentiles with whom he had been banqueting. We cannot suppose that he foresaw the consequence of this act, and that in seeking to avoid offending the one he would scandalise the other. His mistake was no sin, and, according to St. Paul's own teaching, no transgression against the discipline of the Church.

In Acts (xi.) will be seen St. Peter's opinion on the point in question. St. Paul openly expostulates with him to allay the angry feelings of the Gentile converts, and not because he considered the act wrong in itself.

CHAPTER VII.

THE CATHOLIC CHURCH IS THE ONLY TRUE CHURCH.

1. BECAUSE it is governed by the Bishop of Rome, successor to St. Peter, whom Christ appointed ruler of His Church (Matt. xvi. 18).

2. Whether we regard the name Catholic as referring to the time of its existence, or to the number of its adherents, or to its diffusion throughout the world, the Church governed by the Sovereign Pontiff alone merits the name of Catholic. It is Catholic in time, being the only Christian Church in existence when the Apostles issued their creed: 'I believe in the Holy Ghost, the Holy Catholic Church,' and it is the only Church that has come down to us from them. It is Catholic in the number of its followers, for there are far more Catholic Christians than any others. It is Catholic in place, being more diffused throughout the world than any other Christian religion.

3. Its Members are all of one faith, whilst the other Christian sects are divided amongst themselves, and utterly disunited in their belief.

CHAPTER VIII.

THE SACRAMENT OF HOLY ORDER.

I. *Christ instituted a sacred hierarchy of bishops and priests, distinct from laics, to govern His Church.*

ALL Christians are not on an equality in the Church, as from the number of those who were converted Christ specially selected certain men, whom He made 'ministers of the New Testament' (2 Cor. iii. 6).

Moreover, a special vocation is required for the priesthood:

'No man taketh this honour unto himself, but he that is called of God, as was Aaron' (Heb. v. 4).

St. Paul, therefore, says, speaking for himself and the priests of the Church:

'Let a man so account of us, as of the ministers of Christ, and the stewards of the mysteries of God' (1 Cor. iv. 1).

The appointment of bishops is likewise mentioned in the Sacred Scriptures. St. Matthias is elected to the 'bishopric' of Judas (Acts, i. 20); and St. Paul exhorts the newly appointed bishops or overseers:

'Take heed, therefore, unto yourselves, and to all the flock, over the which the Holy Ghost hath made you overseers, to feed the Church of God, which He hath purchased with His own Blood' (Acts, xx. 28).

The virtues that should distinguish the bishops are mentioned:

'If a man desire the office of a bishop, he desireth a good work' (1 Tim. iii. 1).

'A bishop must be blameless,' &c. (1 Tim. iii. 2).

II. *The Apostles ordained priests and bishops, who transmitted their power to others.*

This will be gathered from the following instruction of St. Paul to Titus and Timothy, whom he had made Bishops of Crete and Ephesus:

'Neglect not that gift that is in thee, which was given thee by prophecy, with the laying on of the hands of the presbytery' (1 Tim. iv. 14).

'Wherefore I put thee in remembrance that thou stir up the gift of God which is in thee by the putting on of my hands' (2 Tim. i. 6).

'For this cause left I thee in Crete, that thou shouldest set in order the things that are wanting, and ordain elders in every city, as I had appointed thee' (Titus, i. 5).

The Sacrament of Holy Order. 25

III. *The objections of Dissenters to the Sacrament of Holy Order.*

They quote Luke, xxii. 26, as against what has been urged: 'He that is greatest amongst you, let him be as the younger: and he that is chief, as he that doth serve.' The words themselves, however, clearly recognise a difference in authority and position in the Church, and make known to those who are raised above others in the Church that they are to govern in a spirit of meekness, and not with that despotic power with which 'the kings of the Gentiles' rule their subjects.

Dissenters, again, try to prove that all Christians are priests, by quoting:

'Ye are a chosen generation, a royal priesthood, an holy nation, a peculiar people' (1 Pet. ii. 9).

Christ 'hath made us kings and priests' (Rev. i. 6).

Now God addressed the same titles to the Jews:

'Ye shall be unto me a kingdom of priests, and an holy nation' (Exod. xix. 6).

As the words were spoken to the Jews at large, who, as all confess, had a priesthood distinct from the people, so they can be applied to Christians in a like manner, without destroying the distinction between the priesthood and laity.

Christians and Israelites are alike said to be priests, inasmuch as they can offer spiritual sacrifices to God, and in this sense are so entitled by St. Paul, as will be seen by consulting the fifth verse of the chapter given:

'Ye also, as lively stones, are built up a spiritual house, an holy priesthood, to offer up spiritual sacrifices, acceptable to God by Jesus Christ' (1 Pet. ii. 5).

All the Israelites, too, were priests in the same limited sense:

'The sacrifices of God are a broken spirit: a broken and a contrite heart, O God, Thou wilt not despise' (Ps. li. 17).

IV. *The celibacy of the clergy.*

The Church, wishing her priests to aim at the more perfect state, has decreed that they should not marry. Candidates for the priesthood are submitted to a long and strict probation, and are not ordained priests until they have completed the age of twenty-four years, in order that they may have the opportunity of weighing fully the gravity of the step they are taking.

St. Paul speaks of celibacy as the more perfect state:

'He that is unmarried careth for the things that belong to the Lord, how he may please the Lord' (1 Cor. vii. 32).

'But he that is married careth for the things that are of the world, how he may please his wife' (1 Cor. vii. 33).

For this reason St. Paul chose the state of celibacy for himself, and advised others to follow his example:

'I say to the unmarried and widows, it is good for them if they abide even as I' (1 Cor. vii. 8).

CHAPTER IX.

THE SACRIFICE OF THE MASS.

I. *What the Mass really is.*

IT is the bloodless Sacrifice of the Body and Blood of Christ.

It is a true sacrifice, for Christ is really present under the appearances of bread and wine, and is offered to God for our sins; and a bloodless sacrifice, for He cannot die or suffer any more, and is not really, but mystically, slain; and the sacrifice is perfected, since Christ is not only offered, but consumed. It represents in a bloodless and painless manner the great sacrifice of Calvary, as St. Paul teaches (1 Cor. v. 7): 'Christ, our Passover, is sacrificed for us,' *i.e.*, Christ, under the appearances of the bread and wine of the Passover, is offered for us in Eucharistic Sacrifice. The very altar on which it was offered is mentioned by St. Paul (Heb. xiii. 10): 'We have an altar, whereof they have no right to eat that serve the tabernacle.' We have an altar from which the Jews are excluded.

II. *Holy Mass was foretold by the Prophet Malachi.*

Holy Mass is the sacrifice foretold by the Prophet Malachi, the last of the prophets (Mal. i. 11): 'From the rising of the sun, even to the going down of the same, My Name shall be great amongst the Gentiles; and in every place incense shall be offered unto My Name, and a pure offering; for My Name shall be great among the heathen, saith the Lord of Hosts.'

God was indignant with the priests for offering unworthy sacrifices, and the Prophet foretold that these sacrifices should cease with the Jewish dispensation, but the 'pure offering' of the Gentiles should be sacrificed 'everywhere' from 'the rising of the sun, even to the going down of the same,' to God's greater honour and glory. This 'pure offering' cannot refer alone to the Sacrifice on Calvary, or to the sacrifice of the Last Supper, for it is to be offered up everywhere throughout the universal world until the Judgment Day, 'till He come.'

It is in vain to urge that this 'pure offering' refers to a spiritual oblation, for the prophet alludes to a new sacrifice unknown to the Jews, whereas David (Ps. li. 17) makes it evident that spiritual sacrifices always existed: 'The sacrifices of God are a broken spirit; a broken and contrite heart, O God, thou wilt not despise.'

III. Why Christ is called a Priest according to the order of Melchizedek.

Christ is a priest according to the order of Melchizedek. David represents, in the Psalms (cx. 4), God the Father speaking to the Messiah: 'The Lord hath sworn, and will not repent. Thou art a Priest for ever after the order of Melchizedek,' and St. Paul explained the manner in which our Saviour can be said to fulfil this office (Heb. vii. 24): 'This Man' (Christ Jesus), 'because he continueth for ever, hath an unchangeable priesthood.' He is the principal offerer, the priest, the secondary; and whenever Holy Mass is said, Christ offers Himself in Eucharistic sacrifice for the living and the dead, and will do so until the last day, 'till He come.' Melchizedek, who sacrificed in bread and wine, is a type of Christ. This prophecy is fulfilled whenever Christ offers Himself, by the hands of His priests, in the bloodless sacrifice of the Mass. This sacrifice was not destined to end at the last Supper, or at Calvary: it must be continued for ever.

IV. When was this Sacrifice inaugurated?

On Holy Thursday the Eucharistic Sacrifice was inaugurated, and the Apostles ordained priests. On Holy Thursday, the Feast of the Passover, Christ invited His Apostles to meet Him in a room at Jerusalem, that He might inaugurate the Sacrifice of the 'New Testament' (Luke, xxii. 15): 'He said to them, With desire I have desired to eat this Passover with you before I suffer.' On examining the texts that follow, it will be seen that the Passover Supper, consisting of unleavened bread and wine, was but a preliminary to the mystery of the New Testament, for when supper was over,—

Luke, xxii. 19: 'He took bread and gave thanks, and brake it, and gave it unto them, saying, "This is

The Sacrifice of the Mass. 29

My Body, which is given for you; this do in remembrance of Me."'

Luke, xxii. 20: 'Likewise the cup after supper, saying, "This cup is the New Testament of My Blood, which is shed for you."' In that solemn act Christ declared that the bread which He broke was His Body, and the wine which He consecrated was His Blood. In the words, 'This do in remembrance of Me,' He ordained the Apostles Priests by conferring on them the power of performing the same sacrificial act, as St. Paul plainly indicates.

V. *St. Paul said Mass.*

1 Cor. xi. 23: 'I have received from the Lord that which also I delivered unto you; that the Lord Jesus Christ, the same night in which He was betrayed, took bread.'

1 Cor. xi. 24: 'And when He had given thanks He brake it, and said: "Take eat; this is My Body which is broken for you; this do in remembrance of Me."'

1 Cor. xi. 25: 'After the same manner also He took the cup, when He had supped, saying: "This cup is the New Testament of My Blood; this do ye as often as ye drink it, in remembrance of Me."'

1 Cor. xi. 26: 'For as often as ye eat this bread, and drink this cup, ye do share the Lord's death till He come.'

1 Cor. xi. 27: 'Whosoever shall eat this bread, and drink this cup of the Lord, unworthily, shall be guilty of the Body and Blood of the Lord.'

1 Cor. xi. 28: 'But let a man examine himself, and so let him eat of that bread and drink of that cup.'

1 Cor. xi. 29: 'For he that eateth and drinketh unworthily, eateth and drinketh damnation to himself, not discerning the Lord's Body.'

He describes the Holy Sacrifice of the Mass as showing the 'Lord's death,' and the Blessed Eucharist as the 'Lord's Body.' 'Christ, our Passover, is sacrificed for us.' The Eucharistic Sacrifice is therefore a bloodless representation of the Sacrifice of the Cross.

VI. *The Holy Sacrifice of the Eucharist was offered up to God during the first three centuries.*

Selecting a time when the 'Disciplina Arcani,' or custom of teaching the 'initiated' only the most sacred mysteries of the Christian Faith, when the doctrines of the Catholic Church were necessarily mentioned with the greatest caution, Protestant controversialists frequently challenge Catholic writers to produce evidence from the first ages of the Church to show that Holy Mass was offered up during those times. They also urge, what every Catholic writer admits, that the word 'Mass,' as signifying the Eucharistic Sacrifice, is not to be found during the first three centuries, but the 'oblations' of St. Clement in the first; the 'pure offering' of St. Iræneus and the 'sacrifices' of St. Justin and Tertullian in the second; and the great 'sacrifice' of St. Cyprian, in the third century, can easily be identified with the Eucharistic Sacrifice or Holy Mass, derived from 'ita missa est,' the words used by the priest at the conclusion of the mystery, and generally adopted since the beginning of the fourth century, by the common consent of Christians, to designate one and the same sacred function. For the reason mentioned, the 'Disciplina Arcani,' it would prove nothing either in favour of Protestantism or against Catholicity if all mention of the Eucharistic sacrifice were omitted in the writings of the Fathers of the first three centuries.

The 'initiated' could only, during the first ages, realise the full signification of the cautious expressions which the Fathers made use of to express the meaning of the sacred Christian rites; but now when the words of the early Christians are examined in the full light of faith and freedom, no question can seriously be raised about their true signification.

An Infidel writer, Gibbon (*Decline and Downfall of the Roman Empire*, Vol. I., p. 387), in mentioning the 'Disciplina Arcani,' remarks: 'The precautions with which the disciples of Christ performed the offices of religion were first dictated by fear and necessity, but they were continued from choice. But the event, as it often happens in the operations of a subtle policy, deceived their wishes and expectations. It was concluded that they only concealed what they would have blushed to disclose . . . There were many who pretended to confess or relate the ceremonies of this abhorred society. It was asserted that a newborn infant, entirely covered over with flour, was presented, like some mystic symbol of initiation, to the knife of the proselyte, who unknowingly inflicted many a secret wound on the innocent victim of his error; that as soon as the cruel deed was perpetrated, the votaries drank up the blood; greedily tore asunder the quivering members, and pledged themselves to eternal secrecy by a mutual consciousness of guilt,' &c.

It is not difficult to discover in this a gross distortion of the Doctrine of the Eucharistic Sacrifice, and of the Blessed Eucharist given to the faithful for the food and nourishment of their souls. 'The new-born infant covered with flour' is Christ Jesus under the appearances of bread; and the 'votaries who drank the blood and greedily tore asunder the quivering members' of the infant slain by the proselyte were the early Christians partaking of the body and blood of Jesus Christ. St. Cyprian (*Tract ad Demet*, sect. 7) speaks of the 'Disciplina Arcani':—'Your temples and altars are kept always warm and smoking with your sacrifices; and yet the true God hath no altars, but what we are forced to conceal.' Having before us the reasons why the Fathers of the first three centuries did not explain the doctrines of divine faith more openly, let us closely examine their writings for any evidence tending to show that Holy Mass was offered up to God for the living and the dead during the earliest ages of the Church.

(*a*) *The Sacrifice of the Mass existed in the First Century.*—It has already been shown (1 Cor. xi. 23-29) that St. Paul consecrated and distributed Holy Communion, which he called 'the Lord's Body,' to the faithful, and he called the Eucharistic Sacrifice 'showing the Lord's death,' and this sacrifice consisted in the unleavened bread and wine of the Passover changed into the Body and Blood of Christ: 'Christ our Passover is sacrificed for us' (1 Cor. v. 7); just as the Catholic Church teaches that Holy Mass is a memorial of Christ's passion and death.

(*b*) *The Sacrifice of the Mass in the Second Century.*—St. Justin Martyr (*Dial. cum Tryph.*, N. 41, pp.137, 13), A.D. 130, quotes the Prophet Malachi i. 11, to prove the Eucharistic Sacrifice. 'The oblation of wheaten flour prescribed to be offered to those who were purified from leprosy (Lev. xiv.) was a type of the bread of the Eucharist, which our Lord Jesus commanded us to offer for a commemoration of the Passion, which He endured for those who are purified as to their souls from all the iniquity of men . . . Whence God, as I said, declares of the sacrifices then offered by you, by Malachi, one of the twelve: " My will is not in you, saith the Lord; and your sacrifices I will not receive from your hand; for from the rising of the sun, even to the going down, My Name hath been glorified among the Gentiles, and in every place incense is offered to My Name, and a clean sacrifice, because My Name is great amongst the Gentiles, said the Lord." Even then does he foretell concerning the sacri-

The Sacrifice of the Mass.   33

fices offered unto Him in every place by us Gentiles, that is, of the bread of the Eucharist, and the cup, in like manner, of the Eucharist; saying that His Name is by us glorified, and by you profaned.' The thirty-first of the Thirty-nine Articles calls masses for the living and the dead 'blasphemous fables and dangerous deceits.' Yet Tertullian, born A.D. 160, in that century declared (*De Corona*, N. S., p. 102) that 'we make on one day every year oblations for the dead as for [their] birthdays.'

(*c*) *Holy Mass was Celebrated during the Third Century.*—St. Cyprian, who was born A.D. 200, and suffered martyrdom A.D. 258, will prove this proposition. He is the first writer who speaks most openly in the days of the 'Discipline of the Secret' about the doctrines and liturgy of the Sacrifice of the Mass.

The following quotations are taken from the Oxford translation of his works, republished A.D. 1717 by the Rev. Nathaniel Marshall, LL.B., chaplain-in-ordinary to the Queen. St. Cyprian proves that Jesus Christ by His sacrifice at the Last Supper is a true priest according to the order of Melchizedek (Epistle 63, sect. 2). 'Melchizedek was a priest of the Most High God when he offered up wine and blessed Abraham. And who, I pray, is more properly and truly a Priest of the Most High God than our Lord Jesus Christ? Who offered up a sacrifice to His Father—the very same which Melchizedek had offered before Him, namely, bread and wine, which were His own Body and Blood.' He states that Jesus gave all His priests power to offer up the Eucharistic Sacrifice, or say Mass. (Epistle 63, sect. 6.) 'If Jesus Christ our Lord and God be Himself the great High-Priest of God the Father, and accordingly first offered His own Person as a sacrifice to the Father, and afterwards directed us to do the like in commemoration of Him, then that priest doth most properly represent his Master in this action,

D

keeps most closely to the pattern which Christ hath set him; he then offers up to God the Father, in His Church, the *truest and completest sacrifice*, if he celebrates it in the manner wherein he is assured that Christ Himself did celebrate it.'

St. Cyprian tells us what took place whilst he was saying Mass.

De Lapsis, Sect. 13: 'A woman somewhat advanced in years, who crept in unobserved amongst the communicants when I was offering up the great Sacrifice. She, as soon as she received the holy elements, began to heave and struggle for her life,' &c.

He gives the reason why Mass was said in the morning and not in the evening—because it is more commemorative of the Sacrifice of the Cross, which was offered up in the morning, than of the Sacrifice of the Last Supper.

Epistle 63, sect. 7: ' Some say that our Lord did not offer up the cup thus mixed in the morning, but in the evening and after supper, and that we should celebrate our Lord's Institution after supper, too; and will it not be sufficient if we offer up the cup mixed as He offered it? To which I reply that it behoved Christ to offer towards the close of the evening, that the hour in which He offered this sacrifice might remind us of the world's approach towards its evening, as we find it written in the Book of Exodus, "All the congregation of Israel shall kill in the evening;" and again in the Psalms, "Let the lifting up of my hands be an evening sacrifice." But we celebrate our sacrifices in the morning in honour of our Lord's Resurrection: and because in all our sacrifices we mention the Passion of our Lord (for the *Passion of our Lord is indeed the main of our sacrifice*), we should follow the pattern He has set us in it, since the Scripture saith expressly, that as often as we eat this bread and drink this cup, we shall *show the Lord's death until He come.* Wherefore, if we offer up the cup in commemoration of our Lord's sufferings, let us by all means do what we know Him to have done before us.'

Masses offered for the dead on their anniversaries (Epistle 39, sect. 1): 'We constantly offer, as you remember, sacrifices for them upon the yearly return of those days wherein we celebrate the memorial of the martyrs' sufferings.'

On the reverence with which we should assist at Mass (Lord's Prayer, sect. 3): 'When we meet our brethren together in public congregation, and there join with the priest in the oblation of his heavenly sacrifice, reverence and modesty are particularly then becoming us.'

The reason why the priest at the offertory mixes water with the wine (Epistle 63, sect. 3): 'Now we find that the cup whereof our Lord made His oblation was mixed, and that the wine of it was what He called His blood, from whence it is apparent that the blood of Christ is not offered if the cup hath no wine in it, and that we do not offer up the sacrifice which our Lord commanded in a proper manner unless our oblation and sacrifice correspond with His practice in the first Institution. How, then, shall we drink this wine new in the kingdom of His Father if in this sacrifice we do not offer up the wine which God and Christ have required, and if we do not mix the cup of our Lord according to our Lord's appointment?'

The antiquity of making offerings on entering the Church before Mass (Alms and Good Works, sect. 11): 'Can you, who are rich and flourishing in your circumstances, imagine that you celebrate the Holy Eucharist as you should do, when you have no regard for the Corban? when you come into the Church and scandalously take your part of those provisions to which even the poor communicants have contributed?'

The preface of the Mass mentioned (Lord's Prayer,

sect. 19), 'We may observe of the person who officiates in our public worship that he prepares the minds of his brethren for the holy work upon which they are entering by prefacing his prayer with a " Lift up your hearts " [*Sursum corda*], that so in the answer they are directed to return to him—" We lift them to the Lord "—they may be reminded of their obligation to think of Him only.'

The reverence with which people should attend Mass (Lord's Prayer, sect. 3): 'Whenever we meet our brethren together in public congregation, and there join with the priest in the oblation of his heavenly sacrifice, reverence and modesty are particularly becoming us.'

If the Archbishop of Canterbury in his Cathedral, or the Bishop of London at St. Paul's, openly proclaimed the same doctrines as St. Cyprian, that Jesus Christ at the Last Supper 'offered up to His Father the very same sacrifice which Melchizedek offered before Him, namely, bread and wine, which are His own Body and Blood;' that every priest who stands at God's altar and keeps 'closely to the pattern which Christ hath set Him, offers to God the Father in his Church *the truest and completest sacrifice;*' if either of the Bishops ever said that a poor woman 'crept in unobserved when I was offering the great sacrifice,' and crowned all by proclaiming that 'we constantly offer, as you remember, " sacrifices " for the dead on their anniversaries: every Protestant present in the congregations would cry out that their Lordships had gone over to Rome, and grievously sinned against the 31st Article, which they had sworn to observe, viz.: that Masses offered up for the living and the dead 'are blasphemous fables and dangerous deceits.'

VII. *Holy Mass does not lessen the infinite greatness of the Sacrifice on Calvary.*

Many answer to what has been said, that St. Paul,

The Sacrifice of the Mass. 37

in his Epistle to the Hebrews, denies the necessity of the Mass:

There is no need that Christ 'should offer Himself often' (Heb. ix. 25).

The words refer to the sacrifice on Calvary, as will be seen from verses 15 and 16 of the same chapter, and mean that Christ cannot suffer a painful death again.

Protestants also quote:—

'We are sanctified through the offering of the Body of Christ once for all' (Heb. x. 10).

'After He had offered one sacrifice for sins for ever, sat down on the right hand of God' (Heb. x. 12).

Now, Catholics say they fully believe that all men are sanctified, and pardoned the guilt of their sins, through the efficacy of Christ's death on the Cross, so that they do not need another victim and another Calvary. But though full atonement has been made for the sins of all, and God's anger has been appeased by our Saviour's death, it is necessary that the merits of Christ's atonement should be applied to each in those ways which our Blessed Lord has ordained, viz., by the Sacraments, and by the Sacrifice of the Mass; and without this application of Christ's merits to individuals salvation cannot be obtained; a principle admitted by Protestants, who maintain that though Christ died 'once for all,' faith and baptism are necessary for salvation. It cannot, therefore, be affirmed that the Sacrifice of the Mass is derogatory to the Sacrifice of the Cross, since, according to the teaching of the Catholic Church, it applies to us not any merits of its own, but only those of the Sacrifice of the Cross, of which it is a lasting memorial.

To sum up in a few words, we have an 'unchangeable priesthood' (Heb. vii. 24); Christ's priests have an altar whereon to sacrifice (Heb. xiii. 10); the victim is Christ Jesus, offered once in a bloody manner on the altar of the Cross (Heb. x. 10); now in an unbloody manner, in commemoration of the Sacrifice of the Cross (1 Cor. v. 7; xi. 26), in the Sacrifice of the Mass, as was foretold by the prophet Malachi:

'From the rising of the sun to the going down of the same,' &c. (Mal. i. 11).

CHAPTER X.

WHY LATIN IS USED AT THE DIVINE SERVICE.

1. LATIN has been used in the divine services by the Western Church from the apostolic times.

2. Catholics, by studying the different parts of the divine service, and by reading the prayers translated in their prayer-books, can join with the priest in his prayers, just as well as Protestants can accompany the prayers of their ministers.

3. Having once learned the method of accompanying the priest at Mass, Catholics, when travelling abroad, find themselves perfectly familiar with the services of their Church, which never vary.

4. Arguing from analogy, there is nothing strange in the fact that divine services should be conducted in a language unknown to the people; for the Jews, from the Babylonian captivity to the time of our Lord, conducted their services in a language they had forgotten—the old Hebrew.

5. The custom of saying Mass in Latin stirs up in the people who attend the divine service a greater awe and reverence, and guards them from that familiarity and carelessness which would follow from the introduction of the vernacular.

6. To those who say that St. Paul (1 Cor. xiv.) forbids the use of unknown tongues in the services of the Church, we answer, that he only condemns the abuse of the gift of tongues by some of the disciples in addressing the people in public discourses, and

without an interpreter. St. Paul's prohibition cannot refer to the constant practice of the Church, for, as has been said, the divine services are interpreted for the faithful in their prayer-books.

CHAPTER XI.

THE SACRAMENT OF THE EUCHARIST.

I. *Christ promised that He would give Himself to the faithful in the Blessed Eucharist.*

IT is for no empty display of divine power, but to lead the people to believe in a still greater miracle, that our Saviour (in John, vi.) feeds the five thousand with five loaves and two fishes. He takes occasion of that miracle to instruct the people who follow Him the next day in the mystery of the Eucharist. Gradually He leads them to the truth He is about to enunciate:

'Verily, verily I say unto you, Moses gave you not that bread from heaven; but My Father giveth you the true bread from heaven' (John, vi. 32).

He then seeks to arouse their faith:

'Verily, verily I say unto you, he that believeth on Me hath life everlasting' (John, vi. 47).

'I am that bread of life' (of which He had been speaking) (John, vi. 48).

'Your fathers did eat manna in the wilderness, and are dead' (John, vi. 49).

'This is the bread which cometh down from heaven, that a man may eat thereof and not die' (John, vi. 50).

'I am the living bread which came down from heaven; if any man eat of this bread he shall live for ever: and the bread which I will give is My Flesh, which I will give for the life of the world' (John, vi. 51).

'The Jews, therefore, strove among themselves, saying, How can this Man give us His Flesh to eat?' (John, vi. 52).

Listen to our Saviour's answer:

'Verily, verily I say unto you, Except ye eat of the Flesh of the Son of Man, and drink His Blood, ye have no life in you'* (John, vi. 53).

'Whoso eateth My Flesh and drinketh My Blood hath eternal life; and I will raise him up at the last day' (John, vi. 54).

'For My Flesh is meat indeed, and My Blood is drink indeed' (John, vi. 55).

'He that eateth My Flesh and drinketh My Blood dwelleth in Me, and I in him' (John, vi. 56).

'As the living Father hath sent Me, and I live by the Father; so he that eateth Me, even he shall live by Me' (John, vi. 57).

'This is that bread which came down from heaven: not as your fathers did eat manna, and are dead: he that eateth this bread shall live for ever' (John, vi. 58).

'These things said He in the synagogue, as He taught in Capernaum' (John, vi. 59).

See how our Lord answers the objection of the Jews, 'How can this Man give us His Flesh to eat?' in verses 54–58. And as we cannot conceive Him wilfully confirming them in error, which it would be blasphemy to suppose, it must be acknowledged that He really meant to give Himself to the faithful under the appearance of bread in the Eucharist. 'The bread which I will give is My Flesh, which I will give for the life of the world.'

---

* The phrase, to eat the flesh of another, means in all Oriental languages, when taken figuratively, to calumniate another, as the word 'backbite' means in English. It is, therefore, impossible the Jews should suppose our Lord to be speaking figuratively.

It must be also remarked that the Jews would have no difficulty in believing Him, if He meant communion in the spiritual sense, as they already communicated in this way:

'And did all eat the same spiritual meat' (1 Cor. x. 3).

'And did all drink the same spiritual drink; for they drank of that spiritual rock that followed them, and that rock was Christ' (1 Cor. x. 4).

Now, not only the Jews, but Christ's own disciples, when they knew what He taught, said:

'This is a hard saying; who can hear it?' (John, vi. 60).

'When Jesus knew within Himself that His disciples murmured at it, He said unto them: Doth this offend you?' (John, vi. 61).

'What and if ye shall see the Son of Man ascend up where He was before?' (John, vi. 62).

Then He added:

'It is the spirit that quickeneth; the flesh profiteth nothing' (John, vi. 63).

Christ used these words in explanation of the true doctrine of the Eucharist. In the Communion we receive Christ whole and entire; His Body together with his soul and divinity, and not His Body alone, which would profit nothing.

It is clear, however, that the disciples did not understand these last words to imply a spiritual communion, for

'From that time many of His disciples went back, and walked no more with Him' (John, vi. 66).

'Then Jesus said unto the twelve: Will ye also go away?' (John, vi. 67).

'Then Simon Peter answered Him: Lord, to whom shall we go? Thou hast the words of eternal life' (John, vi. 68).

'And we believe and are sure that Thou art that Christ, the Son of the living God' (John, vi. 69).

II. *Our Saviour fulfilled His promise at the Last Supper.*

'And He said unto them: With desire I have desired to eat this passover with you before I suffer' (Luke, xxii. 15).

'For I say unto you, I will not any more eat thereof until it be fulfilled in the kingdom of God' (Luke, xxii. 16).

'And He took the cup, and gave thanks, and said: Take this, and divide it among yourselves' (Luke, xxii. 17).

'For I say unto you, I will not drink of the fruit of the vine until the kingdom of God shall come' (Luke, xxii. 18).

'And He took bread, and gave thanks, and brake it, and gave it unto them, saying: This is My Body, which is given for you; this do in remembrance of Me' (Luke, xxii. 19).

'Likewise the cup after supper, saying: This cup is the new testament of My Blood, which is shed for you' (Luke, xxii. 20).

St. Luke gives a fuller account of the Last Supper than either St. Matthew or St. Mark, and tells us that our Saviour spoke of the 'fruit of the vine' before the actual institution of the blessed Sacrament. The 'fruit of the vine' refers to the wine of the Paschal feast they were celebrating; whereas the cup after consecration is styled by our Saviour 'the new testament of My Blood.' The marked way in which both are distinguished is one of the strongest proofs of the Real Presence.

III. *The early Christians believed in the Real Presence when they received the Blessed Eucharist.*

St. Paul appeals to the faithful:

'The cup of blessing which we bless, is it not the communion of the Blood of Christ? The bread which

The Sacrament of the Eucharist. 43

we break, is it not the communion of the Body of Christ?' (1 Cor. x. 16.)

With this before their eyes, who can say that the holy bread of the Communion is not the Body, or the consecrated wine the Blood of our Lord?

St. Paul speaks again to the point:

'I have received of the Lord that which also I delivered unto you: That the Lord Jesus Christ, the same night in which He was betrayed, took bread' (1 Cor. xi. 23).

'And when He had given thanks, He brake it, and said: Take, eat; this is My Body, which is broken for you: this do in remembrance of Me' (1 Cor. xi. 24).

'After the same manner also He took the cup when He had supped, saying: This cup is the new testament of My Blood: this do ye, as often as ye drink it, in remembrance of Me' (1 Cor. xi. 25).

'For as often as ye eat this bread, and drink this cup, ye do show the Lord's death till He come' (1 Cor. xi. 26).

Dean Stanley charged the Anglican translators with conscious dishonesty in changing the 'or,' in the original, into 'and' in translating the following verse:

'Whosoever shall eat this bread, and drink this cup of the Lord, unworthily, shall be guilty of 'the Body and Blood of the Lord' (1 Cor. xi. 27).

'But let a man examine himself, and so let him eat of that bread and drink of that cup' (1 Cor. xi. 28).

'For he that eateth and drinketh unworthily, eateth and drinketh damnation to himself, not discerning the Lord's Body' (1 Cor. xi. 29).

Unworthy communicants are condemned for not 'discerning the Lord's Body,' and so profaning our Saviour's Real Presence in the Eucharist.

CHAPTER XII.

NO NECESSITY FOR COMMUNICATING IN BOTH KINDS.

I. *Proof from Scripture that there is no necessity for the faithful to receive Communion in both kinds.*

IN John vi. our Lord speaks only of one kind—consecrated bread—and mentions that one species as containing Himself wholly and completely, as He stood before them :
'I am that Bread of Life' (John, vi. 48).
Mentioning this one kind only, He added :
'Whoso eateth My flesh, and drinketh My Blood, hath life everlasting,' &c. (John, vi. 54).
We receive Christ completely and perfectly in one kind alone. This doctrine is the natural conclusion of that which we hold about the Real Presence. Christ is living, and not dead, in the Eucharist. Where His Body is, there must also be His Blood; and where His Blood is present, under the appearance of wine, His living Body must necessarily be present, and by receiving in one kind we receive a perfect Communion.

The Sacred Scriptures have not left us without examples of communicating in one kind. Our Lord gives Communion in one species to the two disciples whom He meets on the road to Emmaus :
'And it came to pass, as He sat at meat with them, He took bread and blessed it, and brake and gave it to them' (Luke, xxiv. 30).
'And their eyes were opened, and they knew Him; and He vanished out of their sight' (Luke, xxiv. 31).
We read in the Acts of the converts baptized by St. Peter :
'They continued stedfastly in the Apostles'

doctrine and fellowship, and in the breaking of bread, and in prayers' (Acts, ii. 42).

These are the only scriptural examples of communicating the faithful, and in them Communion in one kind alone is mentioned.

II. *Tradition testifies to the sufficiency of receiving Communion in one kind alone.*

We learn from St. Cyprian (*De Lapsis*), and Tertullian (lib. ii. cap. v. *ad uxorem*), that the faithful were wont to carry home with them, on Sundays, particles of the sacred bread sufficient for communicating themselves during the week. Evagrius (lib. iv. c. xxxvi.) informs us that 'it is an old custom in the imperial city, that when there remains a considerable quantity of the holy fragments of the immaculate Body of Christ our God, boys of tender age should be fetched from among those who attend the schools to eat them.' Infants at baptism received in Communion the Precious Blood (St. Cyprian, *De Lapsis*); and the Greeks adhere to this custom to the present time. The sick and dying were communicated with particles of the consecrated bread (Eusebius, book v. cap. xliv.).

The people frequently, in public Communion in church, received only one species. Thus, the Manicheans received Communion in the form of bread alone, because they held that wine was evil in itself. It was to unmask these heretics that Pope Gelasius commanded the faithful to receive under both kinds.

Again, the Greek Church, from the fourth century down to the present, has had the custom of saying Mass of the Præsanctified on all days of Lent except Saturdays, Sundays, and the feast of the Annunciation of the Blessed Virgin; and the Latin Church has, from the fifth century, always offered Mass of the

Præsanctified on Good Friday ; and in each Mass the priest communicates under one form alone.

III. *Objections answered.*

Against the arguments urged in favour of Communion in one kind, some object that the Greeks, on the occasions referred to, moistened the bread with wine before consecration.

This objection is refuted by the fact that no trace of such a custom can be found in the earliest Greek liturgies. It is, therefore, evident that the practice has crept in in later times. Even admitting the great antiquity of the custom, it cannot be adduced by our adversaries in support of their opinions, because the Greeks always dry the bread which they have moistened with wine before consecration. Surely this disproves the necessity of 'drinking the cup of the New Testament,' which our opponents maintain to be of indispensable obligation, by virtue of the command of our Lord.

The truth, therefore, of the Catholic teaching is quite evident : there is no necessity for the laity to communicate in both kinds. I say the laity, because when the priest offers, he must, out of regard to the integrity of the sacrifice, consecrate and receive in both species.

IV. *The Doctrine of Christ's Real Presence in the Holy Eucharist was taught by the Fathers of the First Three Centuries.*

(*a*) First century. St. Ignatius, martyr, a disciple of St. John the Evangelist, appointed Bishop of Antioch A.D. 68, martyred A.D. 107. In his *Epistle ad Smyrn.* n. 7, he denounced the Docetæ because 'they abstain from Eucharist and prayer, because they confess not that the Eucharist is the flesh of our

Saviour Jesus Christ, the flesh which suffered for our sins, which the Father in His mercy raised again.'

(*b*) Second century. Tertullian, born 160, *De Resurrectione Carnis*, n. 8, page 330, writes on the same subject : 'The flesh is fed with the body and blood of Christ, that the soul may be fattened of God.'

(*c*) Third century. Many non-Catholics stoutly maintain that St. Cyprian was a Protestant. It will be advantageous to give his written statement of belief in the Real Presence (Lord's Prayer, sect. 12) : 'Christ is indeed the bread of life, but He is not so to all, but to us only. Wherefore we say our Father, because God is the Father of such as know and believe in Him ; so we call this bread our daily bread, inasmuch as Christ is our bread ;—ours, I say, who stand so nearly related to Him by *a participation of His body*. This bread we desire may be daily given us ; by which we, who are in Christ, and so every day receive the Eucharistical elements for the nourishment of our souls unto eternal life, do express our fear of being separated from Christ by the commission of some heinous sin, which should expose us to the dreadful sentence of excommunication, and thereby deprive ourselves of that bread of heaven. Our Lord himself hath told us, saying, "*I am the bread of life, which came down from heaven ; if any man eat of my bread he shall live for ever*, and the bread which I will give is my flesh, which I will give for the life of the world." When, therefore, He saith, "If any man eat of this bread he shall live for ever," as it is evident that they are actually living who are entitled to *a participation of the holy Eucharist*, and *in that awful rite* receive into their hands *His sacred Body*, so it is a fit subject of our prayer and caution that we may not be separated from *the Body of Christ* by the sentence of excommunication, which would bring us so near the very borders of everlasting ruin, our Lord having warned us to this purpose in His gospel, saying, "*Except ye eat the flesh of the Son of Man, and drink His blood,* ye have no life in you." We desire, therefore, that our bread, viz., Christ, may be daily given us, that *we who live at present and abide in Christ* may go on to do so, may not lose those sanctifying influences which flow from His body, when received by such as are duly entitled to a participation of it.'

Again (*De Lapsis*, sect. 1): 'Your mouths which have been sanctified with the food of heaven, and *with the body* and blood of Christ, would not after that defile themselves with the impure remains of meat offered to idols.' (See genuine works of St. Cyprian, published A.D. 1717, by Nathaniel Marshall, LL.B., chaplain-in-ordinary to the Queen.)

CHAPTER XIII.

THE SACRAMENT OF BAPTISM.

I. *Christ instituted this Sacrament.*

HE commanded the Apostles:

'Go ye therefore, and teach all nations, baptizing them in the name of the Father, and of the Son, and of the Holy Ghost' (Matt. xxviii. 19).

II. *It is absolutely necessary that children, as well as adults, should be baptized.*

Our Lord says, without any distinction whatever:
'Except a man be born of water and of the Spirit, he cannot enter into the kingdom of God' (John, iii. 5).

These words, especially if we take into consideration the force of the Greek text, in which this Gospel

The Sacrament of Baptism.

was written, include all, without regard to age; and from them it can be rightly inferred that there is no ground for the assertion that adults alone can be baptized.

Neither does the want of intention on the child's part prove that infant baptism is invalid; for as in the Jewish Church the faith of the parents or sponsors supplied the want of faith in the child in circumcision, so the want of faith in the child in baptism is supplied by the Church.

Moreover, it is impossible for any one who holds that we are born in original sin to call in question the necessity of infant baptism.

Now, the doctrine of original sin is an article of faith, for the Scriptures teach that every one is born in sin:

'Behold, I was shapen in iniquity, and in sin did my mother conceive me' (Ps. li. 5).

'As by one man sin entered into the world, and death by sin; and so death passed upon all men, for that all have sinned' (Rom. v. 12).

Origen (in *Rom.* book vi. chap. v.), speaking on this question, says:

'For this reason the Church of Christ received it as a tradition from the Apostles to baptize children, since they, to whom the dispensation of the mysteries of Christ was committed, knew full well that all had a taint of original corruption, and therefore stood in need of having it washed away by baptism.'

So necessary is this Sacrament to save all that St. Peter compares it to the ark:

'The like figure whereunto even baptism doth also now save us' (1 Pet. iii. 21).

III. *Baptism by immersion is not necessary.*

Baptism was administered in three ways in the early Church—by immersion, or by pouring water on, or by sprinkling the person to be baptized—and the

Sacrament administered in any of these ways was considered valid.

Baptism by immersion is not necessary, for we read (Acts, xvi. 33) that St. Paul when in prison baptized his jailer and family, which could not have been by immersion, but either by pouring water on or sprinkling them. The sick and the imprisoned were accustomed to be baptized by either of these latter means (*Neander*, Vol. I., p. 429), and were never afterwards rebaptized conditionally.

IV. *What is the fate of infants and heathens who, having faithfully observed the natural law, die unbaptized?*

From what we know of God's justice and mercy, and the express teaching of our Lord (John, xv. 22), it is certain that heathens who have not had the Gospel preached to them, but who have served and worshipped God according to the precepts of the natural law, will not be condemned by a just God to the fire of hell after death. Neither will infants who die unbaptized be condemned; for the fire of hell is always represented in the sacred Scriptures as the punishment of grievous actual sin. Thus:

'Depart from Me, ye cursed, into everlasting fire' (Matt. xxv. 41).

'For I was an hungered, and ye gave Me no meat,' &c. (Matt. xxv. 42).

It is commonly believed that heathens who have not knowingly sinned against God, and unbaptized children, enjoy a natural beatitude in some place such as limbo, where the just who died before Christ were detained.

CHAPTER XIV.

THE SACRAMENT OF PENANCE.

I. *Institution of this Sacrament by Christ.*

'HE breathed upon them, and saith unto them: Receive ye the Holy Ghost' (John, xx. 22).

'Whosesoever sins ye remit, they are remitted unto them; and whosesoever sins ye retain, they are retained' (John, xx. 23).

Our Lord in these words gave the Apostles power to 'forgive or retain' sins; which means that He gave them power to give or refuse absolution, according to the dispositions of the sinner. It is obvious that the words imply a necessity of sacramental confession, as the Apostles could not exercise a proper discretion in the matter of giving or refusing absolution unless the faithful made known their sins to them.

Our Saviour again assures the Apostles:

'Verily, verily I say unto you, whatsoever ye shall bind on earth shall be bound in heaven; and whatsoever ye shall loose on earth shall be loosed in heaven' (Matt. xviii. 18).

St. Paul therefore truly says:

'We are ambassadors for Christ, as though God did beseech you by us; we pray you in Christ's stead be ye reconciled to God' (2 Cor. v. 20).

II. *The Apostles exercised the power of forgiving sins conferred on them by Christ.*

It is stated by St. Paul that

'Many that believed came and confessed, and showed their deeds' (Acts, xix. 18).

That these 'deeds' were sins is evident from the following verse:

'Many of them also which used curious ärts' (that is, who practised sorcery) 'brought their books together and burned them before all men; and they counted the price of them, and found it fifty thousand pieces of silver' (Acts, xix. 19).

The newly received Christians confessed their sins of sorcery, and manifested their purpose of amendment by burning their wicked books.

St. James, too, speaks of the sick confessing their sins to the elders or priests, whom they should call in to attend them!

'Is any sick among you? let him call for the elders of the Church; and let them pray over him, anointing him with oil in the Name of the Lord' (James, v. 14).

'And the prayer of faith shall save the sick, and the Lord shall raise him up; and if he have committed sins, they shall be forgiven him' (James, v. 15).

'Confess your faults one to another, and pray for one another, that ye may be healed' (James, v. 16).

The 'faults,' or transgressions, of last verse correspond with the 'sins' of verse 15. Both verses must be taken in connexion with verse 14, and then it will be seen that the confession is to be made by the sick to their fellow-men, the elders or priests, whom they are commanded to 'bring in,' and by whose prayers they shall 'be healed.'

III. *Confession of sin was practised both in the Old and in the New Testament.*

It was commanded by God that an Israelite who had sinned, or heard the voice of swearing, or contracted even a legal impurity, if 'he shall be guilty of one of these things, that he shall confess that he hath sinned in that thing' (Lev. v. 5).

A specific confession of sin was, therefore, required Again :

The Sacrament of Penance.   53

"When a man or a woman shall commit any sin that men commit, to do trespass against the Lord, and that person be guilty' (Numb. v. 6),
'Then they shall confess the sin which they have done,' &c. (Numb. v. 7).

The people who flocked to hear John the Baptist: 'Were baptized by him in the Jordan, confessing their sins' (Matt. iii. 6).

Finally, God promises pardon to all Christians who confess their sins:

'If we confess our sins, He is faithful and just to forgive us our sins, and to cleanse us from all unrighteousness' (1 John, i. 9).

In the Apostles' Creed, after professing our belief in the Catholic Church, we go on to declare our belief in the forgiveness of sins: and we know from tradition that in the Catholic Church, in the East and in the West, the practice of confessing sins to the ministers of Christ in order to obtain forgiveness has always existed. It is true that, in the early age of the Church, heretics, such as the Montanists, whilst they admitted the obligation of the faithful confessing their sins, denied that the Church had power to forgive certain great crimes, such as apostasy, adultery, &c. But Christ has put no limitation upon the power of the Church: 'Whosesoever sins ye remit, they are remitted.' If this precept of the necessity of confessing our sins to obtain their forgiveness had not come down from apostolic times, but had been introduced into the Church at any later period, it is certain that the whole Christian world would never have, without remonstrance, submitted to so great a change, and equally certain that history would bear witness to the opposition which would have been made in innumerable places to the imposition of such a burden upon the consciences of all the people, without distinction of priests and laymen.

IV. *Confession during the First Three Centuries.*
First Century.
St. Clement of Rome (2 *Epist. ad Cor.*, sect. 18) declares that 'after we have gone out of this world no confession or penance will ever a whit avail us.'
Third Century.
St. Cyprian (*De Lapsis*, sect. 10) states that 'a delusive absolution will be dangerous to the giver and useless to the receiver,' and adds the reason: 'Before they have in any manner endeavoured to satisfy for their offence; before they have made a solemn confession of it.'
And sect. 14 (*idem*) exhorts all Christians, 'Wherefore, my beloved brethren, let every one of you who has offended make an humble confession of his sin, whilst yet in the land of the living, whilst his confession is likely to be available; whilst the satisfaction he endeavours to make for himself, and whilst the intercession of the Priest for his forgiveness, are acceptable to God.'
Again, in speaking of those who apostatised, and were afterwards too easily re-admitted into the Church, he indignantly remarked (Epistle xvi. sect. 1): 'Though the persecution is still raging, and consequently the peace of the Church is not yet settled, they are rashly and hastily admitted to Communion, and their names are solemnly offered to God upon His altar; nay, though they have *not yet performed their penance;* though they have made *no public confession of sin;* though they have received no imposition of hands from the Bishop and his clergy, the Holy Eucharist is administered to them, in the face and, it would seem, in defiance of that Scripture which saith: "Whosoever shall eat the bread, or drink this cup of the Lord unworthily, shall be guilty of the Body and Blood of the Lord"' (1 Cor. xi. 27).

CHAPTER XV.

INDULGENCES.

I. *The meaning of an Indulgence.*

AN indulgence is a remission either altogether or in part of the temporal punishment which remains due to forgiven sin, by the application of the merits of Christ and His saints, made by the Church. A plenary indulgence remits all the punishment due to sins the guilt of which has already been forgiven; and a partial indulgence remits only a certain portion of the same punishment, according to the number of days or years mentioned in the indulgence.

We have an example of this temporal punishment in the penitential works of prayer, alms, or fasting, which are imposed by the priest in the Sacrament of Penance to satisfy God for the sins which have been confessed. We have an example also in the pains inflicted by God in purgatory upon those who have not made sufficient satisfaction in this life.

An indulgence of one year or one hundred days does not mean that they who gain such an indulgence shall be delivered from one year's or one hundred days' suffering in purgatory, but it means that if the faithful perform with due dispositions whatever is enjoined to gain these indulgences, the Church, relying on the power given her by God (Matt. xviii. 18), declares that equivalent to the performance of one year or one hundred days of canonical penance.

II. *A certain amount of temporal punishment frequently remains due to sin when its guilt has been forgiven.*

God forgave the guilt of original sin when Christ died for us on the Cross; He forgave the guilt of the

Israelites in question at the prayer of Moses; but the temporal punishment due to Adam's sin remains (Gen. iii. 17–19); and the Israelites were debarred from ever entering the Promised Land (Numb. xiv. 19–23). King David sinned, and God forgave its guilt in these words :

'The Lord hath put away thy sin' (2 Sam. xii. 13).

But there was nevertheless a punishment inflicted upon that sin :

'The child also that is born to thee shall surely die' (2 Sam. xii. 14).

III. *Our Saviour gave to St. Peter, and to the Apostles and their successors, power to remit both the guilt of sin and also its temporal punishment, for a reasonable cause.*

The following will prove this statement :—

'Verily I say unto you, whatsoever ye shall bind on earth shall be bound in heaven; and whatsoever ye shall loose on earth shall be loosed in heaven' (Matt. xviii. 18).

He gave this same power in like words to St. Peter, as head of the Church :

'And I will give unto thee the keys of the kingdom of heaven: and whatsoever thou shalt bind on earth shall be bound in heaven; and whatsoever thou shalt loose on earth shall be loosed in heaven' (Matt. xvi. 19).

We have already seen that Christ gave the Apostles power to forgive the guilt of sin in His name :

'Whosoever sins ye remit, they are remitted unto them: and whosoever sins ye retain, they are retained' (John, xx. 23).

If these three texts just given be taken together, it will be seen that the Church has not only power of forgiving the guilt of sin, but also of remitting the temporal punishment due to sin; or, in other words, of granting indulgences.

Indulgences.

This may be seen more clearly still by consulting 2 Cor. ii. St. Paul remits, at the request of the faithful, the punishment of excommunication in the case of the incestuous Corinthian, and tells us plainly that in doing so he only exercised that power of forgiving the punishment due to sin conferred on the Apostles by Christ. This is the obvious meaning of the words:

'To whom ye forgive anything, I forgive also; for if I forgave anything, to whom I forgave it, for your sakes forgave I it in the person of Christ' (2 Cor. ii. 10).

The Church, therefore, has the power of granting indulgences, or of remitting the temporal punishment due to forgiven sin, for a reasonable cause. The celebration of the great festivals of Christmas, Easter, Whitsunday, the occurrence of a Jubilee, the necessity of encouraging some pious work, and of inducing the faithful to frequent Confession and Communion, are considered reasonable occasions for granting indulgences.

IV. *By the 'communion of saints' the superabundant satisfaction of Christ and His saints may be applied to the faithful in the form of indulgences.*

We are taught by the 'communion of saints,' and by the Lord's Prayer, which is addressed to 'Our Father' in the name of all His children, that Christians can assist each other by their prayers and good works.

One drop of Christ's Precious Blood was sufficient to redeem the world. In pouring out His life's Blood on Calvary, in fearful agony, He not only paid the price of our ransom, but left us 'a full and plenteous redemption.' His superabundant satisfaction and the satisfaction of the good works performed through the help of His grace by the saints, who endured more than was necessary to satisfy for the temporal punishment due to their own sins, remain at the disposal of the Church, to be applied by her as occasion may arise to the benefit of her children. By participating in the superabundant satisfactions of Christ and His saints, we may then obtain some remission of the temporal punishment which remains due to our sin, provided those sins have been repented of and forgiven.

CHAPTER XVI.

PURGATORY.

I. *All who admit a difference between the guilt of venial and mortal sin are bound to admit a difference in the degree of punishment due to these sins in the next life.*

SEEING how inevitably this conclusion follows, many Protestants who refuse to believe in purgatory refuse consequently to admit of any difference in degrees of guilt; such doctrine, however, leaves the just no greater hope of salvation than the wicked, for St. John says absolutely:

'If we say that we have no sin, we deceive ourselves, and the truth is not in us' (1 John, i. 8).

Again:

'The just man falleth seven times' (Prov. xxiv. 16).

And yet the Psalmist adds;

'Though he fall, he shall not be utterly cast down; for the Lord upholdeth him with His hand' (Ps. xxxvii. 24).

What is the conclusion which follows from these texts? All men, even they who are called just, commit sin. If the teaching of Protestants, then, be true, there exists no real difference between the just and the wicked—between those who commit lesser sins of human frailty, to which all are more or less subject, and the drunkards, adulterers, &c, of whom it is written that they shall not enter the kingdom of God (1 Cor. vi. 9, 10).

Returning once more to the text:
'If we say that we have no sin, we deceive ourselves, and the truth is not in us' (1 John, i. 8).

This may be said of the just, then, at the last moment of their lives, according to the reasoning of Protestants; they are as guilty, therefore, as the greatest sinners when they stand before God. Is not such a conclusion absurd, except the most extravagant doctrine of predestination be maintained?

But there are different degrees of sin. 1 John, v. 16, 17, speaks of 'sins unto death and sins not unto death.' Moses tells the Israelites who fell into idolatry:

'Ye have sinned a great sin,' &c. (Exod. xxxii. 30).

Our Lord declares Judas's sin to be greater than Pilate's:

'He that delivered Me unto thee hath the greater sin' (John, xix. 11).

Blasphemy is greater than other sins (Matt. xii. 31).

We cannot, then, but admit a difference between the sins of the just and the sins of the wicked: the one is saved, the other lost. Now, as nothing defiled can enter God's kingdom, the just must be purified in some way in the life to come. The Apostle says: 'Yet so as by fire' (1 Cor. iii. 15)—not by the fire of hell, for the wicked are punished with 'everlasting fire' (Matt. xxv. 41), but by the cleansing fire of purgatory.

II. *The Jews believed in Purgatory.*

The Jews believed in a temporal state of punishment, which many of the brethren who had avoided certain sins should have to undergo before entering paradise. (See Calmet, *Dictionary of the Bible*.) They believed that their prayers and sacrifices would merit a remission of this punishment, as will be seen by reading 2 Maccabees, xii. 43-46. To avoid all dispute, this book is quoted as a faithful Jewish history. The Jews themselves regarded it as such. It states that Judas Maccabæus made a collection of 12,000 drachmas of silver, and sent it to Jerusalem, that sacrifices might be offered for the soldiers who had fallen in battle, and gives as a reason:

'It is a holy and a wholesome thought to pray for the dead, that they may be loosed from their sins' (2 Maccabees, xii. 46).

Modern Jews repeat their 'Kadisch,' a prayer for the dead; and Bartholoccius (*Bib. Rabbinica*, vol. ii., pp. 149 and 151) testifies to the Jewish belief in the temporal punishment and salvation of many of their brethren who had departed out of this life under the guilt of lesser sin.

III. *Why we pray for the Dead.*

The faithful, taught by the 'communion of saints' that they can assist each other by their prayers and good works, frequently pray and get the Holy Sacrifice offered for the faithful departed, and they beg of God that He may accept their pious acts in the way of satisfaction for those who can no longer merit for themselves—the souls in purgatory.

Therefore St. Paul prayed for Onesiphorus, who was dead: 'The Lord grant unto him that he may find mercy of the Lord in that day' (2 Tim. i. 18).

IV. *Prayers for the Dead.*

Second century.

Tertullian (*De Monog.* N. x., page 531), speaking of a widow praying for her late husband, states:

Purgatory. 61

'Wherefore does she pray for his soul, and begs for him in the interim refreshment, and in the first resurrection companionship, and offers on the anniversary days of his falling asleep.' Origen on the same subject (tom. ii., hom. 6, in Exod., N. 4, page 148): 'For this cause, therefore, he that is saved is saved by fire, that if he happen to have anything in the nature of lead commingled with him, that the fire may burn and melt it away, that all men may become pure gold; because the gold of the land which the saints are to possess is said to be pure; and, as *the furnace trieth gold*, so doth temptation try the just' (Ecclus. ii. 5). 'All, therefore, must come to the fire; all must come to the furnace. For the Lord sits and refines, and He shall purify the sons of Judah (Mal. iii.). 'But also, when we shall have come to that place, if one shall have brought many good works, and some little iniquity, that little is melted away, and purifies in the fire like lead, and all remains pure gold' (compare this with 1 Cor. iii. 12–15).

Third century.

Again, St. Cyprian (1 Epist., sect. 2): 'Wherefore, since Victor, against the express letter of the canon lately made upon this occasion in an assembly of bishops, hath presumed to appoint Germinius Faustinus, a Presbyter of the Church, his executor, you have, we think, no reason to make any oblation for him, nor to offer up, on his behalf, the customary prayers of the Church.'

Epist. 39, sect. 1 : 'We constantly offer up, as you remember, sacrifices for them upon the yearly return of those days wherein we celebrate the memorial of the martyrs' sufferings.'

CHAPTER XVII.

PENITENTIAL GOOD WORKS.

I. *Works of penance prescribed in the Old Testament.*

NOT only were penitential works performed with a view to satisfy for the temporal punishment due to sins which had been forgiven, but we read that the guilt of sin itself was taken away, and God's anger appeased, by works of penance joined with sincere conversion to God.

We read in Exod. xxxiv. 28 that Moses fasted and prayed forty days and forty nights in behalf of the children of Israel, and ceased not until God promised to forgive them. The king of Nineveh, terrified by Jonah's threats, orders a fast for men and beasts; and God, pleased with this self-imposed penance, pardons the fated city. David testifies to the good effect of fasting: 'I humbled my soul with fasting' (Psa. xxxv. 13; lxix. 10); and the prophet Joel implores the people: 'Turn ye . . . . with fasting, weeping, and with mourning' (Joel, ii. 12). See also Gen. xxxvii. 34; 2 Sam. iii. 31; 1 Kings, xx. 31; 2 Kings, xix. 1.

II. *Penitential good works inculcated by our Lord and the Apostles.*

Christ fasted forty days and forty nights (Matt. iv. 2); and tells His disciples that the dumb spirit could only be driven out by 'prayer and fasting' (Mark, ix. 29). The Holy Ghost hears the prayers of the disciples, who 'ministered to the Lord and fasted' (Acts, xiii. 2). St. Paul recommends fasting and prayer to the faithful (1 Cor. vii. 5), and practised this virtue himself (1 Cor. ix. 27). Read also 2 Cor. vi. 5.

The Sacrament of Extreme Unction.

CHAPTER XVIII.

THE SACRAMENT OF EXTREME UNCTION.

I. *The truth of this Sacrament proved from Scripture.*

'Is any sick among you? let him call for the elders of the Church; and let them pray over him, anointing him with oil in the name of the Lord' (James, v. 14).

'And the prayer of faith shall save the sick, and the Lord shall raise him up; and if he have committed sins, they shall be forgiven him' (James, v. 15).

II. *The Apostles anointed the sick.*

'They cast out many devils, and anointed with oil many that were sick, and healed them' (Mark, vi. 13).

We have here the figure of the Sacrament which was instituted at a later time.

III. *The benefits of this Sacrament.*

Christ instituted this Sacrament that, by the anointing and prayers of the priest, the sins of those who are in danger of death by sickness may be forgiven them, and that they may be strengthened to meet death with resignation; or, should their recovery be beneficial to their souls, that they may be restored to health by God.

CHAPTER XIX.

THE BLESSED VIRGIN MARY.

I. *The Blessed Virgin should be honoured by Christians more than any of the angels or saints.*

THE Angel Gabriel, as God's messenger, honours her more than any human creature or angel in heaven has been honoured:

'Hail, thou that art highly favoured, the Lord is with thee; blessed art thou among women' (Luke, i. 28).

St. Elizabeth cries out:

'Blessed art thou among women, and blessed is the fruit of thy womb' (Luke, i. 42).

'Whence is this to me, that the Mother of my Lord should come to me?' (Luke, i. 43).

And the Blessed Virgin, inspired by the Holy Ghost, prophesies:

'Behold, from henceforth all generations shall call me blessed' (Luke, i. 48).

See the respect and reverence of St. Elizabeth in addressing her: 'Whence is this to me that the Mother of my Lord should come to me?'

All who bear in mind that Mary is the Mother of Jesus, and that God has never yet selected any one to carry out His design in this world without conferring on such a person at the same time graces sufficient to accomplish His will, must acknowledge that the Blessed Virgin received more graces from on high than any angel or saint, that she might worthily fulfil her high destiny as Mother of Jesus.

II. *Mary was always a virgin.*

She was a virgin before Christ's birth:

'Behold, a Virgin shall be with child, and shall bring forth a Son; and they shall call His name Emmanuel, which, being interpreted, is, God with us' (Matt. i. 23).

This scriptural assurance, that Mary preserved her virginity when espoused to St. Joseph, before the birth of her Divine Son, is, apart from tradition, a strong argument that she preserved it ever afterwards. God wisely ordained that she should be espoused to the 'just man,' St. Joseph, that Jesus might have a foster-father, and that the Virgin's name should be saved from the calumnies of the Jews.

Some people, misinterpreting the Scriptures, say

that the Blessed Virgin had other children besides Jesus, and they quote :
'His Mother and His brethren stood without' (Matt. xii. 46).

It is only necessary to point out, in answer, that relations are called brethren in Scripture, *e.g.*, Lot and Abraham. James, Joses, and Judas, being relations of our Lord, are called His brethren ; but they were the sons of Cleophas and Mary, who is mentioned as standing by the Cross on Calvary (John, xix. 25).

One more text is often cited by those who affirm that Mary was not always a virgin :
He 'knew her not till she had brought forth her first-born Son' (Matt. i. 25).

Let us examine the meaning of the word 'till,' or 'until :'—

'The Lord said unto my Lord : Sit Thou at My right hand, until I make Thine enemies Thy footstool' (Psa. cx. 1).

It will not be inferred from this that Christ should only sit at the right hand of God whilst His enemies were being overcome. Again :

Noah 'sent forth a raven, which went forth to and fro until the waters were dried up from off the earth' (Gen. viii. 7).

But that raven never returned to the ark.

It is likewise said of the damned :
'Thou shalt by no means come out thence till thou hast paid the uttermost farthing (Matt. v. 26).

But the lost soul can never escape from hell.

The word 'till' in the text, he 'knew her not till,' &c., does not therefore imply that the Blessed Virgin afterwards lost her virginity.

III. *The Immaculate Conception of the Blessed Virgin.*

By the Immaculate Conception of the Blessed Virgin is meant that God had decreed that she who was destined to be the Mother of His Son should not inherit original sin. The Sacred Scripture implies as much when God, in cursing the serpent for having seduced Eve, declares:

'I will put enmity between thee and the woman, and between thy seed and her seed; it' (Catholic version, 'she') 'shall crush thy head, and thou shalt bruise his heel' (Gen. iii. 15).

Compare with this:

'There appeared a great wonder in heaven; a woman clothed with the sun, and the moon under her feet, and upon her head a crown of twelve stars' (Rev. xii. 1).

'And she brought forth a man-child, who was to rule all nations with a rod of iron' (Rev. xii. 5).

The woman obtains two wings of a great eagle to escape from Satan:

'And the dragon was wroth with the woman, and went to make war with the remnant of her seed, which keep the commandments of God' (Rev. xii. 17).

These texts evidently point to the Blessed Virgin, and declare that she should triumph over Satan. As there was no open combat between the Blessed Virgin and Satan, the victory she achieved consisted in her escaping the devil's wiles, and consequently her immunity from every taint of sin, whether actual or original. It surely does not require any great effort of faith to believe that our Blessed Lord should not permit His Mother to be involved in the sin of Adam. We are not left without instances of God bestowing special favours on those whom He loves. St. John the Baptist and Jeremiah were sanctified before their birth:

'Before thou camest forth out of the womb I sanctified thee, and I ordained thee a prophet unto the nations' (Jer. i. 5).

Is there anything unreasonable, then, in supposing that He should confer a greater favour on His Blessed

Mother, and that He should redeem her, not simply from the guilt, but from the law, of original sin? The doctrine of Mary's freedom from all sin was taught by St. Cyprian and Origen in the third century, by St. Augustine in the fifth, and afterwards more especially by St. Bonaventure, St. Anselm, and Duns Scotus.

IV. *The Assumption of the Blessed Virgin.*

The Christians, from the earliest times, firmly believed in the Assumption, or taking up to heaven of the Blessed Virgin's body, soon after her death, by her Divine Son. He did not wish that that pure body, from which He took His own flesh and blood, should be allowed to corrupt in the grave.

Thus reasons St. Augustine in a sermon attributed to him (*Serm. de Assumptione*): 'Did not Christ preserve His Mother immaculate during life? and in death will He not preserve her body from corruption? ... For I cannot conceive that that most sacred body, from which Christ assumed flesh, should be delivered up to worms. The very thought fills me with horror.'

'To-day,' says St. Athanasius, commenting on the Psalm, 'Mary is placed on the right hand of God, as is sung in the Psalm, "A queen hath stood on Thy right hand"' (Psalm xlv. 9).

Juvenal, Bishop of Jerusalem, in a letter quoted by Nicephorus Callistus in his *Ecclesiastical History*, and Eusebius in his *Chronicon*, testify to the belief of the early Christians in the Assumption of the Blessed Virgin.

See Origen on Blessed Virgin, p. 13.

CHAPTER XX.
THE ANGELS.

I. *Different apparitions of angels to men.*

THE name 'angel' signifies a messenger. In this capacity angels appeared to Abram (Gen. xviii.), Lot (Gen. xix.), Jacob (Gen. xxxii.), Moses (Exod. iii.) and Joshua (Josh. v.). The Angel of Death slew the first-born of Egypt (Exod. xii.), and the army of the Assyrians (2 Kings, xix. 35). The Angel Gabriel (Luke, i. 28) tells the Virgin Mary that she is to be the Mother of Christ; and, at the Nativity of our Lord, an angel appears to the shepherds, telling them that their Saviour is born (Luke, ii.), and a host of angels sing their songs of joy; an angel recalls St. Joseph, with the Virgin and Child, from Egypt (Matt. ii. 19); an angel delivered St. Peter from prison (Acts, xii. 7); and, lastly, an angel slew Herod for his impiety (Acts, xii. 23).

II. *Guardian angels.*

The existence of guardian angels is proved from:

'He shall give His angels charge over thee, to keep thee in all thy ways' (Ps. xci. 11).

'They shall bear thee up in their hands, less thou dash thy foot against a stone' (Ps. xci. 12).

The devil, who tempted our Lord, quoted the Psalm just mentioned, to prove to Christ He had a right to expect that His guardian angel would save Him if He cast Himself down from the pinnacle of the Temple:

'If Thou be the Son of God, cast Thyself down; for it is written: He shall give His angel charge concerning Thee,' &c. (Matt, iv. 6).

Our Lord speaks of the guardian angels of the little children:

'Take heed that ye despise not one of these little ones; for I say unto you, that in heaven their angels

The Angels.

do always behold the face of My Father which is in heaven' (Matt. xviii. 10).

St. Paul speaks of the office of these angels:

'Are they not all ministering spirits, sent forth to minister for them who shall be heirs of salvation?' (Heb. i. 14.)

III. *Angels should be honoured.*

When Lot saw the angels he 'rose up to meet them, and bowed himself with his face towards the ground' (Gen. xix. 1). It is said that the very ground where Moses (Exod. iii. 5) and Joshua stood (Josh. v. 15) was sanctified by the angel's presence. We should honour them as the guardians appointed to watch over and save us (Ps. xci. 11; Heb. i. 14).

IV. *Angels know what passes on earth; they bless and pray for us.*

'I say unto you, there is joy in the presence of the angels of God over one sinner that repenteth' (Luke, xv. 10).

'We are made a spectacle unto the world, and to angels, and to men' (1 Cor. iv. 9).

They pray to God on our behalf:

'The angel of the Lord answered and said: O Lord of Hosts, how long wilt Thou not have mercy on Jerusalem, and on the cities of Judah, against which Thou hast had indignation these threescore and ten years?' (Zech. i. 12.)

'And the Lord answered the angel that talked with me with good words and comfortable words' (Zech i. 13).

See likewise Rev. v. 8; viii. 3, 4.

Jacob wrests a blessing from the angel:

'I will not let thee go, except Thou bless me' (Gen. xxxii. 26).

'And he said: Thy name shall be called no more Jacob, but Israel; for as a prince hast thou power with God and with man, and hast prevailed' (Gen. xxxii. 28).

'And Jacob asked him, and said : Tell me, I pray thee, thy name? And he said : Wherefore is it that thou dost ask after my name? And he blessed him there' (Gen. xxxii. 29).

The dying Israel begs his guardian angel to bless Ephraim and Manasseh in these words:

'The angel which redeemed me from all evil bless these lads' (Gen. xlviii. 16).

The angel can speak and interpret God's will to man :

'And Abraham drew near' (the angel) 'and said : "Wilt thou destroy the righteous with the wicked?"' (Gen. xviii. 23).

'And the Lord said : If I find in Sodom fifty righteous within the city, then I will spare all the place for their sakes' (Gen. xviii. 26).

When Abraham sued for a further remission, the angel said :

'I will not destroy it for ten's sake' (Gen. xviii. 32).

To every one who reads carefully the scriptural texts given in this chapter, it will be evident that angels have a charge over us; that angels should be honoured; that they know what passes on earth, and can obtain for us God's blessing and favour; that they minister to our salvation.

V. *Objections answered.*

It has been said by many Protestants that Jacob asked the angel to bless him, because he believed that angel to be God.

Without dwelling on the argument that angels were frequently called by the name of God in the Old Testament, it is only necessary to state that Jacob asked for the angel's blessing, believing him to be but an angel, and before he asked his name.

Moreover, does not Joshua (v. 14) pay religious homage to one who is undoubtedly an angel, being 'the captain of the host of the Lord?'

Again, it is urged that honouring angels is expressly forbidden by St. Paul in Col. ii. 18.

Clement of Alexandria, Tertullian, and Origen (quoted by Calmet, *Dic. of Bible*, under 'Angels') bear witness that certain Jews, together with Simon and Cerinthus, taught that divine honour should be paid to angels, and their mediatorship preferred to that of Christ. It must have been on account of that wicked doctrine that St. Paul warned the Christians.

Finally, Protestants often quote Rev. xix. 10, where an angel refuses the homage of St. John.

It is evident that the angel, from humility, refused the homage of a saint so highly exalted by God; for it cannot be considered that St. John would try to commit an act of idolatry, and, after having been warned, would endeavour to repeat the same offence (Rev. xxii. 8.).

CHAPTER XXI.

SAINTS.

I. *Meaning of the name Saint.*

THE name saint signifies holy. In its scriptural signification it embraces the blessed in heaven, the just in this world, and Christians generally (Eph. i. 1; 1 Cor. i. 2).

II. *Saints, whether in Heaven or on Earth, can pray for us.*

It would be simply multiplying texts to quote passages which prove the efficacy of the prayers of the patriarchs and prophets of old, and the Apostles of the Christian dispensation. Through the prayers of Moses the Amalekites are defeated (Exod. xvii. 11), and God's anger appeased when He is about to destroy the Israelites (Numb. xiv.); God blessed Isaac for Abraham's sake (Gen. xxvi. 24); the Egyptians on account of Joseph (Gen. xxxix. 5); and Solomon is spared because of David's goodness (1 Kings, xi. 12). As Abraham and David were dead when God blessed Isaac and spared Solomon, it is but fair to infer that the prayers of Abraham and David, who were dead, were heard by God on behalf of their sons. God frequently prefers the prayer of others offered for us to our own. Thus God speaks to Job's false friends: 'Go to My servant Job, and offer up for yourselves a burnt offering, and My servant Job shall pray for you; for him will I accept; lest I deal with you after your folly, in that ye have not spoken to Me the thing which is right, like My servant Job' (Job, xlii. 8).

God pardons the whole people of Israel at the prayer of Moses.

St. James declares 'that the effectual fervent prayer of a righteous man availeth much' (James, v. 16).

St. Paul begs the faithful to pray for him (Rom. xv. 30; 2 Cor. i. 11). The same lesson is taught in the Lord's Prayer ('Our Father') and in the 'communion of saints.'

If the prayer of a 'righteous man' is so efficacious when offered to God for us, greater still will be the prayer of those angels who always see the face of God (Matt. xviii. 10), if elicited in our behalf. Then surely the Mother of Jesus has but to ask to obtain the greatest favours for those who 'fly to her patronage.'

III. *The intercession of the saints is not opposed to the mediatorship of Christ.*

St. Paul, when he wrote the words, 'There is one

God, and one Mediator between God and man, the Man Christ Jesus' (1 Tim. ii. 5), could not wish to imply that the intercession of the saints is opposed to the mediatorship of Christ, as he would be plainly contradicting what he taught (Rom. xv. 30; 2 Cor. i. 11). The statement in 1 Tim. ii. 5 must be taken in connexion with the verse that follows, and then Protestants will perceive that the saint is speaking of the Mediator of redemption:

'There is one God, and one Mediator between God and man, the Man Christ Jesus' (1 Tim. ii. 5).

'Who gave Himself a ransom for all, to be testified in due time' (1 Tim. ii. 6).

All Christians admit that there is but one, who ransomed us with the price of His Blood on Calvary —that is, one Mediator of redemption; but, without prejudice to the doctrine of Christ's sole mediatorship of redemption, we may invoke others, both in heaven and on earth, to intercede for us—or, in other words, we may have many mediators of intercession amongst the angels and saints (Zech. i. 12; Rev. v. 8; Matt. xviii. 10). It is no more derogatory to Christ's mediatorship to supplicate the saints to pray for us in heaven than to ask them to pray for us on earth.

IV. *St. Cyprian's exhortation to pray for one another after death.*

Epistle 60, sec. 2: 'Let us agree in remembering each other in the times of peril and distress, and by recommending, *both here and there*, our common interests at the throne of grace, let us endeavour to procure an alleviation of our several burdens; that whosoever of us shall first be favoured by our Lord with a removal hence, let our affection be still expressed for our brethren *in never-ceasing prayers to the Father for them.*'

Nemesianus, Dativus, Felix, and Victor to their brother Cyprian, Epistle 77: 'Let us therefore assist one another by our prayers at the throne of grace: that God and Christ, and *the whole choir of Angels,* may lend us favourable succour when we most shall want them. We most heartily wish your welfare, our master and brother, and beg your remembrance of us.'

CHAPTER XXII.

THE HOLY CROSS AND SACRED RELICS.

I. *The relics of the saints should be honoured, and may be the occasion of God working miracles.*

As we are told that the ground whereon Moses (Exod. iii. 5) and Joshua (v. 15) stood was sanctified by the angel's presence, it does not need any special scriptural texts to prove that the Cross, red with Christ's Blood, is holy. So with relics of holy men.

See the wonders wrought by Aaron's rod (Exod. vii.), and by Elijah's mantle (2 Kings, ii. 13, 14), the dead body of Elisha (2 Kings, xiii. 20, 21), our Lord's garment (Matt. ix. 21, 22), by St. Peter's shadow (Acts, v. 15), and by handkerchiefs and aprons brought from St. Paul's body to the sick (Acts xix. 12).

II. *Miracles did not cease at the death of the Apostles.*

Without dwelling on the well-authenticated miracles which have been wrought in every age, from the time of the Apostles, let us recall the words of Christ, which clearly prove that He intended giving to the Apostles, and to the faithful who should believe in Him, power of working miracles without limitation as to time:

'He that believeth on Me, the works which I do

shall he do also; and greater works than these shall he do' (John, xiv. 12).

Consult Mark, xvi. 17, 18; Luke, x. 17; Matt. xxi. 21.

From these it will be seen that Christ placed no limitation in time to the miracles that should be worked by the faithful who should believe in His name.

CHAPTER XXIII.

SACRED IMAGES.

I. *God never forbade the making of images, but the making of idols.*

THIS will be seen by examining:

'Thou shalt have no other gods before Me' (Exod. xx. 3).

In the verse that follows is explained the meaning of 'no other gods.' God refers to the idols of the Gentiles.

'Thou shalt not make unto thee any graven image, or any likeness of anything that is in heaven above, or that is in the earth beneath, or that is in the water under the earth (Exod. xx. 4).

'Thou shalt not bow down thyself to them, nor serve them; for I, the Lord thy God, am a jealous God' (Exod. xx. 5).

The third and fifth verses qualify the meaning of the words, 'Thou shalt not make unto thee a graven image,' &c., in the fourth, and from both it is clear that it is unlawful to make graven images to be adored as gods or served.* On the other hand, if the prohibition is taken as unqualified and unexplained by verses three and five, sculpture, painting,

* Compare Exod. xx. 4; xxiv. 17; and Lev. xix. 4.

photography, &c., whether referring to sacred subjects or profane, are forbidden by God! To avoid such an absurd conclusion, Protestants say that the prohibition must be taken in a qualified sense; and, driven to make this admission, they boldly assert that the making of sacred images, such as are used in the Catholic Church, is forbidden by God. The answer to this statement will be found in the following section.

II. *God commands and sanctions the making of sacred images.*

Thus He commands Moses:
'Thou shalt make two cherubims of gold, of beaten work thou shalt make them, in the two ends of the mercy-seat' (Exod. xxv. 18).

Amongst the offerings for the tabernacle made by the people we find:
'And every wise-hearted man among them that wrought the work of the tabernacle made ten curtains of twined linen, and blue, and purple, and scarlet; with cherubims of cunning work made he them' (Exod. xxxvi. 8).

God spoke to Moses:
'Make thee a fiery serpent, and set it upon a pole; and it shall come to pass that every one that is bitten, when he looketh upon it, shall live' (Numb. xxi. 8).

That serpent was a figure of Christ (John, iii. 14).

Solomon in constructing his temple:
'Within the oracle he made two cherubims of olive-tree, each ten cubits high' (1 Kings, vi. 23).

'And he overlaid the cherubims with gold' (1 Kings, vi. 28).

'And he carved all the walls of the house round about with carved figures of cherubims, and palm-trees, and open flowers' (1 Kings, vi. 29).

On the doors of the Temple he carved

'Cherubims, and palm-trees, and open flowers' (1 Kings, vi. 35).

God praised Solomon unreservedly for the temple he had made in His honour.

Josephus (*Antiquities of the Jews*, book xiv., chap. ix., sect. 5) relates that the roof of the second temple, renewed by Herod, 'was adorned with sculptures in wood, representing many figures.'

There is nothing, therefore, idolatrous in having sacred images to excite the devotion of the faithful, and bring more vividly before their minds the life and sufferings of our Lord, &c. Hence we find crucifixes, Stations of the Cross, and sacred images adorning the Catholic churches. Christians in the early ages were too poor and persecuted to adorn their churches with paintings and fine sculptures; but even they traced on the walls of the Roman catacombs and of their humble churches rude, but loving, representations of our Lord and His Blessed Mother, &c. When the Church emerged from persecution, Christian sculptors and painters vied with each other in dedicating their talents to the adornment of the temples of religion, in order that the faithful might more vividly realise the sufferings of Christ and the mysteries of their redemption.

CHAPTER XXIV.

THE SACRAMENTALS.

I. *Holy Water.*

WATER has been adopted as a sign of purification in the Old and New Testaments, as the following texts will prove:—

'A clean person shall take hyssop' (a bunch of herbs), 'and dip it in water, and sprinkle it upon all the tent, and upon all the vessels, and upon the persons that were there, and upon him that toucheth a bone, or one slain, or one dead, or a grave' (Numb. xix. 18).

And David prays the Lord:
'Wash me thoroughly from mine iniquity, and cleanse me from my sins' (Ps. li. 2).

'Purge me with hyssop, and I shall be clean; wash me, and I shall be whiter than snow' (Ps. li. 7).

From the New Testament we learn that St. John in his Baptism of Penance (Matt. iii. 6), and Christ when instituting the Sacrament of Baptism (Matt. xxviii. 19), adopted this symbol to denote the internal purification of the soul of the person baptized.

The faithful use water blessed by the Church, both in their own homes and when they enter the church. They are sprinkled with holy water by the priest in preparation for the solemn celebration of the divine mysteries.

Water thus used with faith and devotion will obtain, through the prayers of the Church, pardon for venial offences, and a remission of the punishment due to sin.

II. *Incense.*

Incense is a sweet-smelling gum which was formerly burned by the priests of Israel on a special altar, and is now used by the Catholic Church at her solemn services. It is symbolical of the Divine Presence and of prayer.

It was first used at the divine command:
'Thou shalt make an altar to burn incense upon' (Exod. xxx. 1).

'And when Aaron lighteth the lamp at even, he shall burn incense upon it, a perpetual incense before the Lord throughout your generations' (Exod. xxx. 8).

The smoke of incense ascends before God, and David prays therefore:

The Sacramentals. 79

'Let my prayer be set forth before Thee as incense, and the lifting up of my hands as the evening sacrifice' (Ps. cxli. 2).

The Prophet Malachi foretells that incense should be used with the great Sacrifice of the New Law—the Mass:

'In every place incense shall be offered unto My name and a pure offering; for My name shall be great among the heathen, saith the Lord of Hosts' (Mal. i. 11).

III. *The Agnus Dei.*

The Agnus Dei is made of wax, stamped with an image of the Lamb of God, and blessed on the feast of St. Agnes. The faithful carry it with them as a token of their love for Christ, and to elicit His special protection.

IV. *Medals are used for a similar purpose.*

They have impressed on them an image of our Lord, His Blessed Mother, or some patron saint whose memory we desire to honour.

V. *The Rosary.*

The Rosary signifies a crown of roses, and represents that spiritual crown which the piety of the faithful has made for the Blessed Virgin.

The Rosary is divided into three parts, each of which contains five mysteries.

The first part contains the joyful mysteries, which recall to mind the Annunciation of the Angel Gabriel to the Blessed Virgin; the Visitation of Mary to her cousin, St. Elizabeth; the Nativity or Birth of Christ; the Presentation of the Child Jesus in the Temple; and the Finding of our Lord after His being three days lost.

The second part of the Rosary contains the sorrowful mysteries, viz., Christ's Agony in the

Garden; His being Scourged at the Pillar; Crowned with Thorns; His Carrying the Cross, and His Crucifixion and Death.

The third part, or the glorious mysteries, commemorate Christ's Resurrection, Ascension; the Descent of the Holy Ghost; the Assumption of the Blessed Virgin into Heaven, and her Coronation as Queen of Heaven.

When each mystery has been recalled to mind, the faithful repeat the Lord's Prayer, ten Hail Maries, and one Gloria in honour of the Trinity. The repetition of the 'Hail Mary' ten times at each mystery has occasioned an ill-considered remark that Catholics honour the Blessed Virgin more than God. It will, however, on the other hand, be apparent to every one that the Rosary gives a complete epitome of our Saviour's life. Why do we say the Hail Mary? Because Mary is the Mother of Jesus, and when we repeat that she is 'blessed amongst women' we declare that 'blessed is the fruit of her womb, Jesus.'

From intensity of devotion Christians repeat the same prayer, and there is nothing wrong or unmeaning in repetition, as Christ Himself, repeating the same prayer in His dreadful agony in the garden (Matt. xxvi.), has taught us.

VI. *The Angelus.*

At morning, noon, and evening the Angelus bell is rung, and prayers are said in memory of the great mystery of our Lord's Incarnation, and to honour His Blessed Mother.

'The angel of the Lord declared unto Mary; and she conceived of the Holy Ghost. Hail, Mary,' &c. 'Behold the handmaid of the Lord; be it done unto me according to thy word. Hail, Mary,' &c. 'The Word was made Flesh, and dwelt amongst us. Hail, Mary,' &c.

VII. *The Scapulars.*

The scapulars are made of cloth and worn on the chest and between the shoulders, as a sign of the sweet yoke of servitude to our Lord or His Blessed Mother. The cloth represents the livery of our servitude, and the faithful who wear the scapular bind themselves to recite certain prayers daily, and aim at a more perfect life, and hope that, having devoted their energies to the service of Christ and His Mother, they will, in return, obtain their favour and protection. The use of the scapulars is in harmony with Holy Writ:

'He hath clothed me with the garments of salvation; He hath covered me with the robe of righteousness' (Isa. lxi. 10).

The Catholic Church, established by Christ, and spread throughout the world by the Apostles and their successors, continually offering up to God the bloodless Sacrifice of the Mass, enriched with the Holy Sacraments and Sacramentals, is the True Church of the Protestant Bible.

• END OF PART I.

PART II.

Instruction for Jews and Unitarians.

CHAPTER I.

THE BLESSED TRINITY.

I. *The object of the following chapter.*

THE doctrine of the Blessed Trinity, which is the cardinal doctrine of Christianity, is rejected by Jews and Unitarians, who deny the Divinity of our Saviour, and the distinct personal existence of the Holy Ghost, and teach that there is but one Person in God, viz., the Eternal Father.

All Christians, on the contrary, except Unitarians, believe that in God there are Three distinct Persons, who possess one and the same nature. They teach that God the Son became Incarnate, and not the Father, or the Holy Ghost; and that God the Holy Ghost descended on the Apostles, but not the Father, or the Son, though the Divine Nature which operated is the same. It must also be remembered that the doctrine of the Blessed Trinity is a mystery, which no one can understand, but which every true Christian is bound to believe, because it has been revealed by God, and confirmed by the Incarnation of the Word and the descent of the Holy Ghost upon the Apostles.

From what has been stated the obvious course to be pursued in the following sections will be, in the first place, to disprove the assertion of the Jews that there is no evidence of the Blessed Trinity in the Old Testament; and, again, of the Unitarians, who maintain that no such doctrine can be anywhere found in the sacred writings.

II. *Examination of the assertion made by the Jews, viz., that the doctrine of the Blessed Trinity cannot be gathered from the Old Testament.*

The first chapter of Genesis will sufficiently refute such a groundless statement :

'God said : Let Us make man in Our image, after Our likeness' (Gen. i. 26).

'So God created man in His own image' (Gen. i. 27).

The words 'Let Us make' evidently suggest more than one Divine Person ; 'in Our image' points to the Unity of the Divine Nature; for the words 'Let Us make' cannot be taken as the plural of eminence, as such a figure of speech is altogether excluded from the Hebrew language.

Many Unitarians, realising what has been urged, have maintained that God addressed Himself to angels, by whom, they say, He made the world and created man. But is it not unnatural to suppose that the great God would thus speak to angels on terms of equality, especially when not one single reason can be given to prove that the angels took any part in the work of creation? The heavens and the earth, on the contrary, are mentioned as the work of God's own hand (Ps. viii. 3 ; cii. 25) ; and it was not the angels, but 'God created man in His own image.' To whom, then, did the Eternal Father speak? David and Isaiah unravel the mystery when they state that the Word and Holy Spirit assisted the Father in the work of creation.

'Thus saith the Lord, thy Redeemer, and He that formed thee from the womb : I am the Lord, that maketh all things, that stretcheth forth the heavens alone, that spreadeth abroad the earth by Myself' (Is. xliv. 24).

'Thou sendeth forth Thy Spirit ; they are created, and Thou renewest the face of the earth (Ps. civ. 30).

'By the word of the Lord were the heavens made ; and all the host of them by the breath of His mouth' (Psa. xxxiii. 6).

God the Father was, therefore, assisted by God the Word and the Holy Spirit in the creation of the world ; and He spoke to them when He said, 'Let Us make man in Our image.'

III. *Refutation of Unitarians, who hold that the doctrine of the Blessed Trinity can nowhere be discovered in the Sacred Scriptures, and that there is but One Person in God, viz., the Eternal Father.*

The following texts contain clear and distinct proofs of the Blessed Trinity :

'Go ye, therefore, and teach all nations, baptizing them in the name of the Father, and of the Son, and of the Holy Ghost' (Matt. xxviii. 19).

'The Comforter, which is the Holy Ghost, whom the Father will send in My name ; He shall teach you all things, and bring all things to your remembrance, whatsoever I have said unto you' (John, xiv. 26).

'There are three that bear record in heaven, the Father, the Word, and the Holy Ghost; and these Three are One' (1 John, v. 7).

If the words in St. Matthew (xxviii. 19) be taken grammatically, they necessarily signify that there are Three distinct Persons in One God. We should not have in the Greek the repetition of the article before both Father, and Son, and Holy Ghost if they were all names of one and the same Person. The Unity of the Divine Nature is expressed by the words, 'In the name.'

St. John (xiv. 26) plainly declares that the Comforter sent by the Father is a different Person from the Father, by whom He is sent, and from the Son, who prays for His coming. The Son, moreover, is evidently represented as a different Person from the Father, to whom He addressed His prayer, and from the Holy Ghost, who is to perfect His work of redemption.

Lastly, St. John distinctly states (1 John, v. 7) that 'the Father, the Word, and the Holy Ghost are One' God.

IV. *The Divine Persons are each One of Them said to be God.*

Thus, the Father is truly God.

Christians have never questioned His divinity; and it is sufficiently declared in Eph. i. 3; John, v. 18.

The Son is truly God.

'Behold, a Virgin shall conceive and bear a Son, and shall call His name Immanuel' (Isa. vii. 14).

'And it shall be said in that day' (when the Saviour shall come), 'Lo, this is our God: we have waited for Him, and He will save us; this is the Lord: we have waited for Him; we will be glad and rejoice in His salvation' (Isa. xxv. 9).

'In the beginning was the Word; and the Word was with God, and the Word was God' (John, i. 1).

The Holy Ghost is truly God.

He is the author of our spiritual regeneration (John, iii. 5); and because He is God the faithful are commanded not to grieve Him by sin (Eph. iv. 30); and fearful punishment will be inflicted on those who blaspheme His sacred name (Matt. xii. 31). He inspired the prophets (Isa. xlviii. 16; Acts, i. 16) and teachers of the Church (John, xiv. 26). He is all-wise (1 Cor. ii. 10); and of Him it is said:

'There are diversities of operations, but it is the same God which worketh all in all' (1 Cor. xii. 6).

'All these things worketh that one and self-same Spirit, dividing to every man severally, as He will' (1 Cor. xii. 11).

And Ananias, who 'told a lie to the Holy Ghost,' is reproached by St. Peter (Acts, v. 4): 'Thou hast not lied unto man, but unto God.'

The Father, the Word, and the Holy Ghost are, therefore, Three distinct Persons, but One and the same God.

CHAPTER II.

THE INCARNATION OF GOD THE SON.

I. *What the Catholic Church teaches about the Incarnation of Jesus Christ.*

IT is an article of faith that the Word or Son of God, who existed from eternity with the Father and the Holy Ghost, assumed in time another nature—the nature of man; and that, consequently, in Jesus Christ there are two natures and two wills, but only one Person. Christ Jesus, therefore, as God, is equal with the Father in all things, but as man He is less than God. Our Lord refers to His human nature whenever He speaks of Himself as less than God, and to His divine when He claims equality with God the Father. If this distinction be once realised, all difficulties about the Incarnation will be solved. 'Had they' (the Unitarians) 'been more acute,' as Dr. Moehler remarks (*Symbolism*, vol. ii. p. 331), 'they must have discerned that, if the Gospel represents the Son as a Person, and at the same time as God (and this they do not pretend to deny), no other relation between Him and the Father is conceivable but that which the Catholic Church has from the beginning believed.'

II. *The opponents of the doctrine of the Incarnation.*

The Jews, in their evident anxiety to deny the divinity of Jesus Christ, whom they have rejected, refuse to admit the divinity of the Messiah, for whose coming they await.

In the apostolic times the Docetæ, whilst admitting the divinity, denied the humanity, of our Lord, and maintained that only in appearance, and not in reality, He assumed human nature, suffered, and died.

Others, like Cerinthus, taught that 'Jesus was not born of a Virgin, but was the Son of Joseph and Mary; that He excelled all others in justice, prudence, and wisdom ; that Christ, after His baptism, descended into Him in the form of a dove, from that principality which is over all ; that He preached the unknown Father, worked miracles, and at last flew back from Jesus; that Jesus rose again, but that Christ remained impassible, being spiritual' (Irenæus, lib. i. cap. xxv.).

The followers of Ebion agreed with the Cerinthians in denying the divinity of Jesus, but refused to admit that Christ descended into Him after His baptism, and departed from Him at His death. In the fourth century the Arians were condemned at the Council of Nice for denying the eternal existence of the Son of God, and for asserting that He was not of the same nature with God the Father. The Socinians of the sixteenth century, together with modern Unitarians, deny the divinity of our Lord. They hold that the Son of God 'is a mere man, who was conceived by the Holy Ghost, and therefore called the Son of God. He enjoyed the distinction, they further teach, of having been, prior to His entrance upon His office, admitted into heaven, where He received the commission relative to mankind. On account of His obedience, they say, He was, after the consummation of His work of redemption, exalted to divine dignity and honour, and all things were made over to Him; so that Christians may turn with confidence to Him, and may adore Him—nay, are bound to do so' (Moehler, *Symbolism*, vol. ii. chap. v.).

III. *It remains, in the first place, to prove from the Old Testament, in opposition to the opinion expressed by modern Jews, that the Messiah whom they expect is called God, and that a twofold generation, eternal and temporal, is ascribed to Him by their own sacred writers.*

Such is the obvious teaching of the following:—

'Thus saith the Lord, thy Redeemer, and He that formed thee from the womb: I am the Lord, that maketh all things, that stretcheth forth the heavens alone, that spreadeth abroad the earth by Myself' (Isa. xliv. 24).

'And it shall be said in that day' (when the Messiah shall come), 'Lo, this is our God: we have waited for Him and He will save us; this is the Lord: we have waited for Him; we will be glad and rejoice in His salvation' (Isa. xxv. 9).

'For unto us a Child is born, unto us a Son is given; and the government shall be upon His shoulder; and His name shall be called Wonderful, Counsellor, the Mighty God, the everlasting Father, the Prince of Peace' (Isa. ix. 6).

Mark, likewise, the doctrine of His twofold generation:

'But thou Beth-lehem Ephratah, though thou be little among the thousands of Judah, yet out of thee shall He come forth unto me that is to be ruler in Israel; whose goings forth have been from of old, from everlasting' (Mic. v. 2).

'Behold, a Virgin shall conceive and bear a Son,

The Incarnation of God the Son.

and shall call His name Immanuel'—that is, 'God with us' (Isa. vii. 14).

IV. *St. John's refutation of the errors of the Docetæ, Cerinthians, and Ebionites evinces the belief of the Apostles both in the divinity and sacred humanity of Jesus Christ.*

'In the beginning was the Word; and the Word was with God, and the word was God' (John, i. 1).

'All things were made by Him' (the Word), 'and without Him was not anything made that was made' (John, i. 3).

'And the Word was made Flesh, and dwelt among us (and we beheld His glory, the glory as of the only-begotten Son of the Father), full of grace and truth' (John, i. 14).

'And I knew Him not; but He that sent me to baptize with water, the same said unto me: Upon whom thou shalt see the Spirit descending and remaining on Him, the same is He which baptizeth with the Holy Ghost' (John, i. 33).

'And I saw, and bear record that this is the Son of God' (John, i. 34).

'And, looking upon Jesus as He walked, he saith, Behold the Lamb of God' (John, i. 36).

The Apostle argues to the same effect in his epistle:

'Whosoever believeth that Jesus is the Christ is born of God' (1 John, v. 1).

'This is the victory that overcometh the world, even our faith' (1 John, v. 4).

'Who is he that overcometh the world but he that believeth that Jesus is the Son of God?' (1 John, v. 5).

'This is He that came by water and blood, even Jesus Christ; not by water only, but by water and blood' (1 John, v. 6).

'For there are Three that bear record in heaven,

the Father, the Word, and the Holy Ghost'; and these Three are One' (1 John, v. 7).

'And there are three that bear witness in earth, the spirit, the water, and the blood; and these three agree in one' (1 John, v. 8).

'If we receive the witness of men, the witness of God is greater; for this is the witness of God, which He hath testified of His Son' (1 John, v. 9).

St. John absolutely declares that every true Christian is bound to believe 'that Jesus is the Son of God,' in opposition to the errors of the Docetæ, who denied His sacred humanity, and of the Cerinthians, who maintained that Jesus was a mere man, on whom Christ descended after His baptism, and departed from Him before His death. St. John lays down that Jesus was Christ and truly God, being made manifest of His baptism; and, when He died, not by water only, but by water and blood.

The Spirit or Holy Ghost in verse 7 must not be taken as identical with the spirit in verse 8. SS. Athanasius and Augustine teach that the spirit in the latter verse refers to the last dying breath of our Lord when He 'gave up the ghost' (John, xix. 30); and 'the water and blood' to that which issued from His side, opened by the soldier's lance (John, xix. 34), both of which prove that Jesus is truly man.

On the other hand, the Father, the Word, and the Spirit in verse 7 testified at Christ's baptism that He is truly God. That testimony is given by St. Matthew (iii. 16):

'And Jesus, when He was baptized, went up straightway out of the water; and lo, the heavens were opened up unto Him, and He saw the Spirit of God descending like a dove, and lighting upon Him.'

'And lo, a voice from heaven saying: This is My beloved Son, in whom I am well pleased' (Matt. iii. 17).

Nor is the testimony of the Incarnate Word wanting : ' Jesus answered and said unto them : Though I bear record of Myself, yet My record is true, for I know whence I came and whither I go ; but ye cannot tell whence I come and whither I go ' (John, viii. 14).

Hence the Father, the Holy Ghost, and our Lord Himself testify to His divinity ; and the water and blood, together with our Lord's last breath, bear witness to His sacred humanity.

V. *An answer to the doctrine of modern Unitarians, who teach that Christ had no eternal existence as the Word of God before He was born of the Blessed Virgin; that He is a mere man, and that honour is due to Him only on account of the work of redemption.*

As all Unitarians profess to believe in our Lord as the Redeemer, it seems somewhat strange that they should be blind to the fact that He claims for Himself an existence as God before He was born of the Blessed Virgin.

He asked the Jews :

'What think ye of Christ ? Whose son is He? They say unto Him : The son of David' (Matt. xxii. 42).

'He saith unto them : How, then, doth David in spirit call Him Lord, saying' (Matt. xxii. 43) :

'The Lord saith unto my Lord : Sit Thou on My right hand till I make Thine enemies Thy footstool?' (Matt. xxii. 44).

'If David called Him Lord, how is He his son ?' (Matt. xxii. 45).

'And no man was able to answer Him' (Matt. xxii. 46).

Christ, however, fully explains Himself in another place :

'Jesus said unto them : If God were your Father, ye would love Me, for I proceeded forth and came from God; neither came I of Myself, but He sent Me' (John, viii. 42).

'Art Thou greater than our father Abraham, which is dead, and the prophets are dead? Whom makest Thou Thyself?' (John, viii. 53).

'Your father Abraham,' answered Jesus, 'rejoiced to see My day; and he saw it and was glad' (John, viii. 56).

Then said the Jews unto Him: Thou art not forty years old, and hast Thou seen Abraham?' (John, viii. 57).

'Jesus said unto them: Verily, verily I say unto you, before Abraham was I am' (John, viii. 58).

These texts show that our Saviour claims for Himself an existence before He was born of the Virgin Mary: 'I proceeded forth from God.' 'He sent Me.' 'Before Abraham was I am.' Only God Himself could use this latter expression—the same He made use of when He sought to teach the people of Israel the doctrine of His eternal existence:

'And God said unto Moses: I AM THAT I AM. And He said: Thus shalt thou say unto the children of Israel, I AM hath sent me unto you' (Exod. iii. 14).

St. Paul also speaks of Christ as of Him by whom 'God hath made the worlds' (Heb. i. 2); and St. John (i. 2), 'All things were made by Him.'

He deserved the worship of angels even before the redemption, for when the Infant Saviour was born God commanded (Heb. i. 6), 'Let all the angels of God worship Him.' And Christ implies that before He was born into the world He was glorified by the Father in heaven.

'I have glorified Thee on earth, I have finished the work which Thou gavest Me to do' (John, xvii. 4).

'And now, O Father, glorify Thou Me with Thine own self, with the glory I had with Thee before the world was' (John, xvii. 5).

And after the Ascension the beloved disciple heard the 'voices of angels, saying:'

'Worthy is the Lamb that was slain to receive power, and riches, and wisdom, and strength, and honour, and glory, and blessing' (Rev. v. 12).

'And every creature which is in heaven and on earth and under the earth, and such as are in the sea, and all that are in them, heard I saying: Blessing, and honour, and glory, and power be unto Him that sitteth upon the throne, and unto the Lamb for ever and ever' (Rev. v. 13).

Therefore 'all men should honour the Son, even as they honour the Father' (John, v. 23).

CHAPTER III.

THE HISTORY OF THE MESSIAH AS FORETOLD BY THE PROPHETS.

I. *His genealogy* (a) *from the seed of Abraham*, (b) *the house of Israel*, (c) *the tribe of Judah and family of David.*

(*a*) FROM the seed of Abraham:

'In thy seed shall all the nations of the earth be blessed' (Gen. xxii. 18).

(*b*) The house of Israel:

'I shall behold Him, but not nigh: there shall come a star out of Jacob, and a sceptre shall rise out of Israel, and shall smite the corners of Moab, and destroy all the children of Seth' (Numb. xxiv. 17).

(*c*) From the tribe of Judah and family of David:

'Behold the days come, saith the Lord, and I will raise unto David a righteous Branch; and a King shall reign and prosper, and shall execute judgment and justice in the earth' (Jer. xxiii. 5).

II. *The time fixed for the Saviour's coming*
(a) *by Israel*, (b) *by Daniel*, (c) *by Haggai.*

(*a*) Israel declares that the Messiah should come at that time when the sceptre of supreme power and authority over the Jewish nation should have passed away for ever from the hands of Judah.

'Judah, thou art he whom thy brethren shall praise; thy hand shall be in the neck of thine enemies, thy father's children shall bow down before thee' (Gen. xlix. 8).

'The sceptre shall not depart from Judah, nor a lawgiver from between his feet, until Shiloh come; and unto Him shall the gathering of the people be' (Gen. xlix. 10).

(*b*) The prophet Daniel gives the exact date when this great event should be expected:

'Seventy weeks are determined upon thy people, and upon thy holy city, to finish transgression, and make an end of sins, and to make reconciliation for iniquity, and to bring in everlasting righteousness, and to seal up the vision and prophecy, and to anoint the Most Holy' (Dan. ix. 24).

'Know ye, therefore, and understand, that from the going forth of the commandment to restore and build Jerusalem, unto Messiah the Prince, shall be seven weeks and threescore and two weeks; the street shall be built up again, and the wall even in troublous times' (Dan. ix. 25).

'And after threescore and two weeks shall Messiah be cut off, but not for Himself; and the people of the prince that shall come shall destroy the city and the sanctuary, and the end thereof shall be with a flood: and unto the end of the war desolations are determined' (Dan. ix. 26).

'And he shall confirm the covenant with many for one week; and in the midst of the week he shall cause the sacrifice and the oblation to cease, and for

as foretold by the Prophets. 95

the overspreading of abominations he shall make it desolate, even until the consummation, and that determined shall be poured upon the desolate' (Dan. ix. 27).

The weeks mentioned cannot refer to weeks of days, for evidently the events enunciated could not, and did not, occur in so many weeks of days. They are not to be taken as weeks of jubilees, for Jerusalem was destroyed and the Jews scattered before two weeks of jubilee could have elapsed.

The weeks, therefore, are prophetical weeks, or weeks of years; and in less than seventy weeks of years the different events recorded by the prophet must have taken place. There were four royal decrees concerning Jerusalem and the temple: (1) the first issued by Cyrus, B.C. 536; (2) the second by Darius, B.C. 519; (3) the third by Artaxerxes, B.C. 458; (4) the fourth by Artaxerxes, again B.C. 455 (Nehem. vi. 15). It is more probable that the prophecy of Daniel dates from this last decree (455 B.C. = 299 after the foundation of Rome). Add 69 weeks of years, *i.e.*, 483 years to 299, and the result is 782 after the foundation of Rome. Now, St. Luke tells us that the Baptist commenced his ministry in the fifteenth year of Tiberius Cæsar (*i.e.*, 782 from the foundation of Rome). Since, then, the public life of our Lord began soon after the commencement of the Baptist's ministry, it must have commenced about 782 B.C.

There can be no doubt, therefore, but that the edict of Artaxerxes was the edict foretold by Daniel. Bearing this in mind, the interpretation of the prophecy is evident. Four hundred and eighty-three years, or seven weeks and sixty-two weeks of years, should elapse between the edict of Artaxerxes and the public appearance of the anointed Saviour to undertake the work of redemption, which corresponds with A.D. 30. One week of year, the seventieth, is still to be accounted for. In the midst of that week or about

A.D. 33, Christ should be slain. After His death a prince, with his people, should come and destroy the city of Jerusalem and the Temple. Then terrible punishments should be inflicted on the Jews for having slain the Messiah.

(c) The sign given by the prophet Haggai by which the Jews might know when the Messiah has come. Haggai prophesied that the second Temple should be glorified by the Saviour's presence; consequently the Messiah must have come before that Temple was destroyed.

'Who is left among you' (the elders of Israel) 'that saw this house' (the Temple) 'in her first glory, and how do you see it now? Is it not, in your eyes,' (the second Temple), 'in comparison of it' (Solomon's), 'as nothing?' (Hag. ii. 3).

'Yet now be strong, O Zerubbabel, saith the Lord; and be strong, O Joshua, son of Josedech the high-priest; and be strong, all ye people of the land' (Hag. ii. 4).

'For thus saith the Lord of Hosts, yet once it is a little while, and I will shake the heavens and the earth, and the sea and the dry land' (Hag. ii. 6).

'And I will shake all nations, and the desire of all nations shall come; and I will fill this house with glory' (Hag. ii. 7).

'The glory of this latter house' (the second Temple) 'shall be greater than of the former' (Solomon's), 'saith the Lord of Hosts; and in this place will I give peace' (Hag. ii. 9).

III. *The prophecies which foretold to the Jews* (a) *that the Messiah should be born of a Virgin,* (b) *at Bethlehem,* (c) *that the God-made Man should appear as a little Child,* (d) *and be adored by kings;* (e) *likewise that He should be called the anointed Saviour or Jesus Christ.*

(a) The Messiah should be born of a Virgin:

as foretold by the Prophets.

'Behold, a Virgin shall conceive, and bear a Son, and shall call His name Immanuel' (Isa. vii. 14).

(*b*) At Bethlehem:

'But thou Beth-lehem Ephratah, though thou be little among the thousands of Judah, yet out of thee shall He come forth unto me that is to be ruler in Israel; whose goings forth have been from old, from everlasting' (Mic. v. 2).

(*c*) The God-made Man should first appear as a little Child:

'Unto us a Child is born, unto us a Son is given; and the Government shall be upon His shoulder; and His name shall be called Wonderful, Counsellor, the Mighty God, the Everlasting Father, the Prince of Peace' (Isa. ix. 6).

(*d*) He should be adored by kings:

'The kings of Tarshish and of the isles shall bring presents; the kings of Sheba and Seba shall offer gifts' (Ps. lxxii. 10).

'Yea, all kings shall fall down before Him; all nations shall serve Him' (Ps. lxxii. 11).

(*e*) The Messiah should be called Christ Jesus or the anointed Saviour:

'I am the Lord thy God, the Holy One of Israel, thy Saviour' (Isa. xliii. 3).

'The kings of the earth set themselves, and the rulers take counsel together, against the Lord and against His anointed' (Ps. ii. 2).

IV. *Prophecies foreshadowing the Saviour's public life:* (a) *a messenger should go before Him;* (b) *the Saviour should preach the Gospel to every one;* (c) *He should work miracles;* (d) *and should ride into Jerusalem in poverty, and seated upon an ass, hailed by the people as their king.*

(*a*) A messenger should go before Him:

'Behold, I will send My messenger, and he shall prepare the way before Me' (Mal. iii. 1).

H

(*b*) The Saviour should preach the Gospel to every one:

'The Spirit of the Lord is upon Me, because the Lord hath anointed Me to preach good tidings unto the meek; He hath sent Me to bind up the brokenhearted, to proclaim liberty to the captives, and the opening of the prison to them that are bound' (Isa. lxi. 1).

(*c*) He should work miracles:

'The eyes of the blind shall be opened, and the ears of the deaf shall be unstopped' (Isa. xxxv. 5).

'Then shall the lame man leap as an hart, and the tongue of the dumb shall sing' (Isa. xxxv. 6).

'I, the Lord, have called Thee,' &c. (Isa. xlii. 6).

'To open the blind eyes, to bring out the prisoners from the prison' (Isa. xlii. 7).

(*d*) The Saviour should ride into Jerusalem in poverty, sitting upon an ass, and hailed by the people as their king:

'Rejoice greatly, O daughter of Zion; shout, O daughter of Jerusalem; behold, thy King cometh unto thee: He is just, and having salvation; lowly, and riding upon an ass, and upon a colt the foal of an ass' (Zech. ix. 9).

V. *The circumstances attending the Saviour's death:*
(a) *He should be sold for thirty pieces of silver,*
(b) *and should suffer an ignominious death for the sins of man;* (c) *an eclipse should occur at his death.*

(*a*) He should be sold for thirty pieces of silver:

'They weighed for my price thirty pieces of silver' (Zech. xi. 12).

(*b*) The Messiah should suffer an ignominious death for the sins of men:

'They shall look upon Me whom they have pierced' (Zech. xii. 10).

'And one shall say unto Him: What are these

wounds in Thine hands? Then He shall answer:
Those with which I was wounded in the house of My
friends' (Zech. xiii. 6).

'He was wounded for our transgressions, He was
bruised for our iniquities; the chastisement of our
peace was upon Him, and with His stripes we are
healed' (Isa. liii. 5).

'All we like sheep have gone astray; we have
turned every one to his own way; and the Lord hath
laid on Him the iniquity of us all' (Isa. liii. 6).

'He was oppressed, and He was afflicted, yet He
opened not His mouth; He is brought as a lamb to
the slaughter, and as a sheep before her shearers is
dumb' (Isa. liii. 7).

'He was taken from prison and from judgment,
and who shall declare His generation? For He was
cut off out of the land of the living; for the transgressions of My people was He stricken' (Isa. liii. 8).

'Therefore will I divide Him a portion with the
great, and He shall divide the spoil with the strong,
because He hath poured out His soul unto death;
and He was numbered with the transgressors' (Isa.
liii. 12).

(c) An eclipse should take place at His death:
'Shall not the day of the Lord be darkness and
not light, even very dark, and no brightness in it?'
(Amos, v. 20).

VI. *The events subsequent to the Messiah's death:*
(a) *He should rise from the dead,* (b) *ascend into heaven,* (c) *and be placed at the right hand of God.*

(a) He should rise from the dead:
'Thou wilt not leave My soul in hell, neither wilt
Thou suffer Thine Holy One to see corruption' (Ps.
xvi. 10).

'His rest shall be glorious' (Isa. xi. 10).

(b) And ascend into heaven:

'Lift up your heads, O ye gates: and be ye lift up, ye everlasting doors; and the King of Glory shall come in' (Ps. xxiv. 7).

'Who is the King of Glory? The Lord strong and mighty, the Lord mighty in battle' (Ps. xxiv. 8).

'Lift up your heads, O ye gates; even lift them up, ye everlasting doors; and the King of Glory shall come in' (Ps. xxiv. 9).

'Who is this King of Glory? The Lord of Hosts, He is the King of Glory' (Ps. xxiv. 10).

(c) The Saviour should then be placed on the right hand of God:

'The Lord said unto my Lord: Sit Thou at My right hand until I make Thine enemies Thy footstool' (Ps. cx. 1).

CHAPTER IV.

JESUS CHRIST IDENTIFIED AS THE MESSIAH.

I. *Their genealogies correspond.*

'THE book of the generation of Jesus Christ, the son of David, the son of Abraham,' &c. (Matt. i. 1).

II. *The time of Christ's coming corresponds with the dates given* (a) *by Israel*, (b) *by Daniel*, (c) *by Haggai.*

(a) Israel prophesied that the taking away of the sceptre of authority over the Jewish nation from Judah should be a sign that the Messiah had come. When Christ was born, that sceptre had departed from Judah, for Herod, an Idumean by birth, ruled over Israel; and thirty-seven years after Christ's death the Sanhedrim, the last vestige of Jewish authority, was swept away. The advent of Christ,

Jesus Christ identified as the Messiah.

therefore, corresponds with the sign given by the dying patriarch, by which the Israelites might know that the Saviour had come.

(*b*) The date fixed by Daniel for the coming of the Messiah had elapsed A.D. 30, when Christ publicly appeared to the Jews, and was baptized by St. John in the Jordan and began to preach salvation to the world. A little more then three years after His baptism, which corresponds with the midst of the last week of years of Daniel, our Divine Saviour was crucified; for He died March 20, A.D. 33. By His death He put an end to the Jewish sacrifices, which henceforth ceased to find favour with God. In the year of our Lord 70, Titus, a Roman general, with his army, besieged Jerusalem, resolving to subdue that fated city by famine and the sword. Of the Jews within the city at the time Josephus writes (*Wars of the Jews*, b. vi. cap. iii.): 'Now, of those who perished by famine in the city the number was prodigious, and the miseries they underwent were unspeakable.' To add to their misery they saw the Temple that they loved burned to the ground. And when Titus entered the city, and gazed on the vast strength of the fortifications, he exclaimed, as Josephus in the same book informs us: 'We have certainly had God for our assistant in this war; and it is no other than God that ejected the Jews out of these fortifications; for what could the hands of men or any machines do towards overthrowing these towers?'

Daniel prophesied that God should make Jerusalem 'desolate, even until the consummation, and that determined shall be poured upon the desolate.' Josephus fills up the description: 'The number of those who were carried captive during this whole war was estimated to be 97,000, as was the number of those who perished during the whole siege 1,100,000.'

'The entire nation' (of the Jews) 'was shut up by Fate as in a prison, and the Roman army encompassed the city when it was crowded with inhabitants; accordingly the number of those that therein perished exceeded all the destruction that either man or God ever brought upon the world' (*ibid.*). Such was the destruction of Jerusalem, prophesied by Daniel; and every word of his prophecy has been terribly realised.

(*c*) The sign given by the prophet Haggai was fulfilled before the destruction of the second Temple, which was to be glorified by the Saviour's presence. The Jews in the Talmud speak of the Temple built by Zerubbabel, and afterwards restored by Herod, as the second Temple. Jesus Christ glorified that Temple by His presence (John, ii. 14). Its destruction soon after His death certainly implied that He was the promised Saviour. If not, where, then, is that Saviour who must have come before the Temple was destroyed? No one but Christ Jesus claimed to be the Saviour; and in vain the Jews look for another Messiah, the time for whose coming has long since passed. The prophet, moreover, assures the people that 'in a little while' the Saviour should come; but more than 2000 years have passed away, and no other Saviour but our Divine Lord has appeared.

III. *Christ Jesus* (a) *was born of a Virgin* (b) *at Bethlehem*, (c) *and appeared as a little Child;* (d) *received the adoration of kings from the East,* (e) *and was called the anointed Saviour or Jesus Christ.*

(*a*) 'Now the birth of Jesus Christ was on this wise: when as His Mother Mary was espoused to Joseph, before they came together, she was found with child of the Holy Ghost' (Matt. i. 18).

'Now all this was done that it might be fulfilled which was spoken of the Lord by the prophet, saying' (Matt. i. 22):

'Behold, a Virgin shall be with child, and shall

Jesus Christ identified as the Messiah.

bring forth a Son; and they shall call His name Emmanuel, which, being interpreted, is "God with us"' (Matt. i. 23).

(*b*) At Bethlehem:
'And Joseph also went up from Galilee, out of the city of Nazareth, into Judea, unto the city of David, which is called Bethlehem' (Luke, ii. 4).

'To be taxed with Mary his espoused wife, being great with child' (Luke, ii. 5).

'And she brought forth her first-born Son, and wrapped Him in swaddling clothes, and laid Him in a manger, because there was no room for Him in the inn' (Luke, ii. 7).

(*c*) Christ first appeared as a little Child:
The angels said unto them (the shepherds): 'Behold, I bring you good tidings of great joy, which shall be to all people' (Luke, ii 10).

'For unto you is born this day in the city of David a Saviour, which is Christ the Lord' (Luke, ii. 11).

'Ye shall find the Babe wrapped in swaddling clothes, lying in a manger' (Luke, ii. 12).

(*d*) He was adored by wise men, or kings, from the East:
'When Jesus was born in Bethlehem of Judea, in the days of Herod the king, behold there came wise men from the East to Jerusalem' (Matt. ii. 1);

'Saying: Where is He that is born King of the Jews? for we have seen His star in the East, and are come to worship him' (Matt. ii. 2).

'And when they were come into the house they saw the young Child, with Mary His Mother, and fell down and worshipped Him; and when they had opened their treasures, they presented unto Him gifts; gold, and frankincense, and myrrh' (Matt. ii. 11).

(*e*) The Holy Child was called Jesus Christ:
'And Jacob begat Joseph, the husband of Mary, of whom was born Jesus, who is called Christ' (Matt. i. 16).

Jesus Christ identified as the Messiah.

The meaning of 'Jesus' is 'Saviour,' and of 'Christ' 'the Anointed.'

IV. *The public life of Christ is identical with that prophesied of the Messiah:* (a) *a messenger preceded Him;* (b) *Jesus preached salvation to the world,* (c) *and worked many miracles;* (d) *He rode into Jerusalem seated upon an ass, hailed by the people as their king.*

(*a*) A messenger preceded Him, viz., St. John the Baptist:
'Behold, I send My messenger before Thy face, which shall prepare Thy way before Thee' (Matt. xi. 10).

(*b*) Jesus Christ preached salvation to the world:
'The Spirit of the Lord is upon Me, because He hath anointed Me to preach the Gospel to the poor; He hath sent Me to heal the broken-hearted, to preach deliverance to the captives, and recovering of sight to the blind, to set at liberty them that are bruised' (Luke, iv. 18).
'To preach the acceptable year of the Lord' (Luke, iv. 19).

(*c*) He worked many miracles:
He raised to life the widow's son (Luke, vii. 14); Jairus' daughter (Matt. ix. 25); and Lazarus (John, xi. 43, 44); He cures a lame man (John, v. 8); heals the deaf and dumb (Mark, ix. 25); restores sight to the blind (Matt. ix. 30); cures the dropsy (Luke, xiv. 4).

Publius Tertullus wrote to Tiberius Cæsar a description of our Lord: 'There appeared in these our days a man of great virtue named Jesus Christ, who is yet living among us, and of the Gentiles is accepted for a prophet of truth; but His own disciples call Him the Son of God. He raiseth the dead to life, and cureth all manner of diseases,' &c.

Jesus Christ identified as the Messiah. 105

(*d*) He rode into Jerusalem sitting upon an ass, hailed by the people as their king:

'And on the next day much people that were come to the feast, when they heard that Jesus was coming to Jerusalem (John, xii. 12), took branches of palm-trees, and went forth to meet Him, and cried: Hosanna! Blessed is He that cometh in the name of the Lord' (John, xii. 13).

'And Jesus, when He found a young ass, sat thereon, as it is written' (John, xii. 14):

'Fear not, daughter of Sion; behold, thy King cometh, sitting on an ass's colt' (John, xii. 15).

V. *The circumstances attending Christ's death are the same as the Messiah's:* (a) *Jesus was sold by Judas for thirty pieces of silver;* (b) *He was put to an ignominious death;* (c) *an eclipse took place at His death.*

(*a*) Jesus was sold by Judas for thirty pieces of silver:

'Judas Iscariot went unto the chief priests' (Matt. xxvi. 14), 'and said unto them: What will ye give me, and I will deliver Him unto you? And they covenanted with him for thirty pieces of silver' (Matt. xxvi. 15).

(*b*) Jesus Christ died an ignominious death:

'They took Jesus and led Him away' (John, xix. 16); 'and He, bearing His Cross, went forth into a place called the place of a skull, which is called in the Hebrew Golgotha' (John, xix. 17).

'And they crucified Him, and two other with Him; on either side one, and Jesus in the midst' (John, xix. 18).

(*c*) An eclipse took place at Christ's death:

'And it was about the sixth hour, and there was a darkness over all the earth until the ninth hour' (Luke, xxiii. 44). 'And the veil of the Temple was rent in the midst' (Luke, xxiii. 45).

106 Jesus Christ identified as the Messiah.

This fact is confirmed by a heathen historian.

Phlogon (*Chron. Alex.*, p. 209) writes : 'One of the greatest eclipses ever witnessed took place in the fourth year of the two hundred and second Olympiad. The darkness was such on the sixth hour of that day that the very stars were seen in the heavens. All Bithynia was shaken by earthquakes, and they devastated the greater portion of the city of Nicæa.' The fourth year of the two hundred and second Olympiad corresponds with the year of our Lord 33.

VI. *The events subsequent to Christ's death:* (a) *He rose from the dead,* (b) *and ascended into heaven;* (c) *It is evident, therefore, that Jesus Christ is the true Messiah, and now stands at the right hand of God.*

(*a*) He rose from the dead :

The angels said to the women who sought the body of Christ :

'Why seek ye the living among the dead ?' (Luke, xxiv. 5). 'He is not here, but is risen. Remember how He spake unto you when He was yet in Galilee' (Luke, xxiv. 6), 'saying: The Son of Man must be delivered into the hands of sinful men, and be crucified ; and the third day rise again' (Luke, xxiv. 7).

(*b*) He ascended into heaven :

'And it came to pass, while He blessed them He was parted from them, and carried up into heaven' (Luke, xxiv. 51).

(*c*) We should therefore conclude that the vision of St. Stephen is true, and that Christ stands at the right hand of God :

'He, being full of the Holy Ghost, looked up stedfastly into heaven, and saw the glory of God, and Jesus standing on the right hand of God' (Acts, vii. 55).

APPENDIX.

A PROFESSION OF CATHOLIC FAITH.

I, *N. N.*, with a firm faith believe and profess all and every one of those things which are contained in that Creed which the Holy Roman Church maketh use of, viz., 'I believe in one God, the Father Almighty, Maker of heaven and earth, of all things, visible and invisible; and in one Lord Jesus Christ, the only-begotten Son of God; and born of the Father before all ages; God of God; Light of Light; true God of true God; begotten, not made; consubstantial to the Father, by whom all things were made. Who for us men, and our salvation, came down from heaven; and was incarnate by the Holy Ghost of the Virgin Mary, and was made man. Was crucified also for us under Pontius Pilate: He suffered and was buried. And the third day He rose again, according to the Scriptures: He ascended into heaven; sits at the right hand of the Father, and is to come again with glory to judge the living and the dead; of whose kingdom there shall be no end. And in the Holy Ghost, the Lord and Life-giver; who proceeds from the Father and the Son; who, together with the Father and the Son, is adored and glorified; who spoke by the prophets. And (I believe) one Holy, Catholic, and Apostolic Church: I confess one Baptism for the remission of sins: and I look for the resurrection of the dead, and the life of the world to come. Amen.'

I most steadfastly admit and embrace apostolical and ecclesiastical *Traditions*, and all other observances and constitutions of the same Church,

I also admit the Holy *Scriptures* according to that sense which our holy Mother the Church has held, and does hold; to whom it belongs to *judge* of the true sense and interpretation of the Scriptures. Neither will I ever take and interpret them otherwise than according to the unanimous consent of the Fathers.

I also profess that there are truly and properly *seven Sacraments* of the new law, instituted by Jesus Christ our Lord, and necessary for the salvation of mankind, though not all for every one: to wit, *Baptism, Confirmation, Eucharist, Penance, Extreme Unction, Orders,* and *Matrimony;* and that they confer grace; and that, of these, *Baptism, Confirmation,* and *Order* cannot be reiterated without sacrilege. I also receive and admit the received and approved *ceremonies* of the *Catholic Church,* used in the solemn administration of all the aforesaid Sacraments.

I embrace and receive all and every one of the things which have been defined and declared in the holy Council of *Trent* concerning *original sin* and *justification.*

I profess, likewise, that in the Mass there is offered to God a true, proper, and propitiatory sacrifice for the living and the dead: and that in the most holy Sacrament of the *Eucharist* there is *truly, really,* and *substantially* the *Body* and *Blood,* together with the *Soul* and *Divinity,* of our Lord Jesus Christ: and that there is made a conversion of the whole substance of the bread into the Body, and of the whole substance of the wine into the Blood; which conversion the *Catholic Church* calls *Transubstantiation.* I also confess that under *either kind* alone Christ is received whole and entire, and a true Sacrament.

I constantly hold that there is a *purgatory,* and that the souls therein detained are helped by the suffrages of the faithful.

Likewise that the *saints,* reigning together with Christ, are to be honoured and invocated, and that

Appendix. 109

they offer prayers to God for us, and that their *relics* are to be had in veneration.

I most firmly assert that the *images* of Christ, of the Mother of God, ever Virgin, and also of the other saints, ought to be had and retained, and that due honour and veneration is to be given to them.

I also affirm that the power of *indulgences* was left by Christ in the Church, and that the use of them is most wholesome to *Christian* people.

I acknowledge the *Holy, Catholic, Apostolic Roman Church* for the mother and mistress of all Churches; and I promise true obedience to the *Bishop of Rome*, successor to St. Peter, Prince of the Apostles, and Vicar of Jesus Christ.

I likewise undoubtedly receive and profess all other things which the sacred canons and general councils, and particularly the holy Council of Trent and the Œcumenical Vatican Council, have delivered, defined, and declared, and in particular about the supremacy and infallible teaching of the Roman Pontiff. And I condemn, reject, and anathematise all things contrary thereto, and all heresies which the Church has condemned, rejected, and anathematised.

I, *N. N.*, do at this present freely profess and sincerely hold this true Catholic faith, without which no one can be saved; and I promise most constantly to retain and confess the same entire and unviolated, with God's assistance, to the end of my life.

THE END.

www.ingramcontent.com/pod-product-compliance
Lightning Source LLC
Chambersburg PA
CBHW031349160426
43196CB00007B/792